TOUCH WOOD

TOUCH WOOD

Meeting the Cross in the
World Today

DAVID RUNCORN

DARTON, LONGMAN AND TODD
LONDON

First published in 1992 by
Darton, Longman and Todd Ltd
89 Lillie Road, London SW6 1UD

ISBN 0–232–51943–9

A catalogue record of this book is available
from the British Library

The scriptural quotations are taken from
The Holy Bible, New International Version
© 1978 by New York International Bible Society

Cover design: Sarah John

Phototypeset in 10/12pt Bembo by Intype Ltd, London
Printed and bound in Great Britain at the
University Press, Cambridge

to the
family
of
St Stephen's church with whom
in the joy and pain
of
shared
life
I
touch
wood

Contents

Contents

Part D — The Wildness of God

'he is not here, he is risen!'

Acknowledgements

Despite the solitary name on the final cover all books are, in fact, community projects. This one is no exception.

As such I owe thanks to the congregation of St Stephen's church. They not only allowed their vicar time to write, but by their energy and enthusiasm they constantly stretch and challenge my own faith and Christian understanding. The thoughts and reflections of the following pages have the shape they do because of the community in which I pray and worship and share life. I wouldn't have it any other way, and it is to them that I dedicate this book with love and thanks!

Various people have kindly sheltered me at various stages of writing – Dr Pam Burdon, Tom and Faith Lees (and the Post Green Community, Dorset), Thelma and Mike Pugh (and so, unwittingly, the British Coal Board Training College in Buckinghamshire!). Bishop Stephen Verney kindly gave his permission for the reproduction of Scilla Verney's picture of the cross on page 28 and Suzanna Rust redrew it for this book. Morag Reeve, at DLT, has again been a most supportive editor.

Finally, Simon Kingston read the text more closely than should be decently required of any reader. His unique way of making trenchant criticism feel like a compliment was certainly more than I deserved, frequently rescued a flagging text – and always encouraged me to keep going.

Monsignor Quixote's Dream

He dreamt that Christ had been saved from the Cross
by the legion of angels to which on an earlier occasion
the Devil had told Him that He could appeal. So there
was no final agony, no heavy stone which had to be
rolled away, no discovery of an empty tomb. Father
Quixote stood there watching on Golgotha as Christ
stepped down from the Cross triumphant and
acclaimed. The Roman soldiers, even the Centurion,
knelt in his honour, and the people of Jerusalem poured
up the hill to worship Him. The disciples clustered
happily around. His mother smiled through her tears
of joy. There was no ambiguity, no room for doubt
and no room for faith at all. The whole world knew
with certainty that Christ was the Son of God.

It was only a dream, of course it was only a dream,
but none the less Father Quixote had felt on waking
the chill of despair. He had found himself whispering,
'God save me from such a belief.'[1]

PART A

Open Arms

'he opened wide his arms for us on the cross'

1

Divine Welcome

' . . . he opened wide his arms for us on the cross'[1]

This is one of my favourite lines from the Anglican Communion service. But the picture it often brings into my mind is not a very pious one. It is a television commercial for British Rail. An Inter-city train has pulled in to the station from a distant destination. A girl steps off the train. She is weary. Then she looks down the platform and her face lights up. There is her loved one waiting to greet her, his arms opened wide for her, an expression of sheer delight on his face. They embrace (cue: orchestra). I don't imagine the Liturgical Commission had this association in mind as they worked on this text but I have ceased to feel guilty. Maybe we are most truly spiritual when we allow our humanity into our religion and let it puncture our solemnity.

Open arms express welcome and greeting. Here is a picture of a journey completed, of longing fulfilled. It speaks of love offered at incredible cost. It reawakens the hope of love received – being held in the embrace of God. There on my knees, in the Holy Eucharist, British Rail can reduce me to tears.

But the deeper question haunts me. What kind of welcome

is so longed for, so costly to arrange, that it can only be offered by arms stretched wide on a cross?

Out of eternity

The story of the cross of Christ begins with God, not with us. 'This is love', says John, 'not that we loved God, but that he loved us and sent his Son as an atoning sacrifice for our sins' (1 John 4:10). It is a vital starting place for all who want to understand the Christian faith. Without the knowledge that 'this is love' the cross is a fearful and violent place to draw near.

On Ash Wednesday, the beginning of Lent, the Church traditionally prays this special prayer.

> Almighty and everlasting God,
> you hate nothing that you have made,
> and forgive the sins of all those who are penitent.
> Create and make in us new and contrite hearts
> that, lamenting our sins
>   and acknowledging our wretchedness,
> we may receive from you, the God of all mercy,
> perfect forgiveness and peace;
> through Jesus Christ our Lord.[2]

What an amazing affirmation: 'you hate nothing that you have made'. It is hard to take that in. Look across the front page of any newspaper and repeat that statement after every news item. Look into your own heart and life. Nothing hated?

Our experience of human love contradicts this. Love does run out. People do change their minds and reject others. But there is no rejection in the heart of God. And God's love is such that in the face of all that is wrong and broken and resistant to his grace, he still draws near in hope. He never gives up on his world. There is still the possibility of change and new life for all that he has made.

We need constantly to take in this truth. Without the knowledge that at the heart of God's attitude to this world is love and not hatred, all our guilt will never find forgiveness, all our repentance will never find mercy. All our disciplines and self-denial for Christ will be a longing to earn acceptance rather than a joyful response to grace. There is no more wearying and self-destructive way of searching for love. Any discipline in the name of religion that is entered without the affirmation of divine love will become a wilderness of self-punishment not purification.

The Christian journey of faith begins and ends in love.

The bit of God that we saw

'Anyone who has seen me has seen the Father', said Jesus to those who asked him what God was like (John 14:9). His whole life was a revealing of the love and ways of the unseen God. In life and ministry he was saying, 'If you want to know what God is like then watch me. We are one. I act as he acts, I love as he loves. I teach from his heart, I follow his will, I grieve as he grieves and suffer as he suffers.'

An early creed in Colossians states this quite explicitly: 'He [Christ] is the image of the invisible God . . . For God was pleased to have all his fullness dwell in him and through him to reconcile to himself all things, whether things on earth or things in heaven, by making peace through his blood, shed on the cross' (Col. 1:15, 19–20).

The cross of Christ reveals, in time, God's eternal character and purpose. This is the way God loves all that he has made. He utterly gives himself for its good and its salvation. God knows no other way of loving. On the cross of Christ, God is simply 'being himself'. It is this truth that transforms the terrible cross of Christ into a celebration of a tree of glory.

There on the first Good Friday, in a quarry outside Jerusalem, we glimpse the glory, power and vulnerability of divine love. There God proclaims his mercy and welcome and his total sharing of the sufferings of the world.

But that isn't a belief we come easily to in a world like ours. In Helen Waddell's novel of the famous medieval love story, Peter Abelard struggles with this belief. As so often an unexpected encounter provokes the biggest questions of all. Walking in the woods he has come across a rabbit, shrieking in pain in a poacher's trap. As his friend watches, he releases it and holds it in his arms.

It lay for a moment breathing quickly, then in some blind recognition of the kindness that had met it at the last, the small head thrust and nestled against his arm, and it died.

It was the last confiding thrust that broke Abelard's heart. 'Thibault,' he said, 'do you think there is a God at all? Whatever has come to me, I earned it. But what did this one do?'

Thibault nodded. 'I know,' he said. 'Only – I think God is in it too.'

'In it? Do you mean that it makes Him suffer, the way it does us?'

Again Thibault nodded.

'Then why doesn't he stop it?'

'I don't know,' said Thibault. 'Unless – unless it's like the Prodigal Son. I suppose the father could have kept him at home against his will. But what would have been the use? All this', he stroked the limp body, 'is because of us. But all the time God suffers. More than we do.'

Abelard looked at him, perplexed. 'Thibault, do you mean Calvary?'

Thibault shook his head. 'That was only a piece of it – the piece we saw – in time. Like that.' He pointed to a fallen tree beside them, sawn through the middle. 'That dark ring there, it goes up and down the whole length of the tree. But you only see it where it is cut across. That is what Christ's life was; the bit of God that we saw. And we think God is like that because Christ was like that, kind, and forgiving sins and healing people. We think that God is like that for ever, because it happened once, with Christ. But not the pain. Not the agony at the last. We think that stopped.'

'Then, Thibault,' Abelard said slowly, 'you think that all this,' he looked down at the little quiet body in his arms, 'all the pain of the world, was Christ's cross?'

'God's cross', said Thibault. 'And it goes on.'[3]

If Thibault has understood rightly, then it must be that we are all much closer to the cross than we realise. In daily, ordinary life, in its joys and pains, God approaches us with the same self-giving love we meet at the cross. And when we approach the cross, the open arms of Christ, we are meeting the love that, however dimly perceived, over-shadows all our ways through this uncertain world.

In this profound and simple way we live with the cross all the time. It is not just Christian faith that is cross-shaped. This cross is not just for 'religious' people. Life itself is cross-shaped. The cross is the 'shape' of God's love – the love in which all things have their beginning and their end without end. The cross reveals the secret which sustains all things.

Fragments of faith

Pilgrims to the Holy Land or other sacred shrines could once buy pieces of the 'real' cross. Indeed the power of such relics to awaken spiritual hunger and focus our devotion can be clearly seen in the recent interest in the Turin Shroud, believed to be the burial shroud of Jesus. Such fragments and relics were a means of prayer and veneration – by means of fragments, drawing near the whole.

In the longing for a faith that is 'in touch' we may attach ourselves to church buildings, to particular liturgies, to certain rituals. None of this is wrong. But they are all fragments of the whole.

When we contemplate the cross of Christ we are always living with fragments. Not literal splinters of wood, but fragments of understanding, glimpses of heart, mind and experience. As long as we recognise they are only fragments they can help us. If we claim the fragment for the whole we are in trouble. Far too much theology of the cross attempts to 'explain it'. But when faith is explained it ceases to be faith. And when God is 'explained', God ceases to be the true God.

Our fragments will bring us so far and that is their gift. But we must know when to set them down or they will keep us from the real meeting. We must be willing to explore the unfamiliar and the uncomfortable . . . to stray beyond our own boundaries of faith and practice.

Follow me

This exploring is more than a generous ecumenical idea. It is a necessity. The cross of Christ was the sincere work of godly men and women. God was killed in the name of God. It was the fruit of a particular type of religious certainty – a faith that holds a fragment and claims it as the whole. It is terribly important that we see our beliefs for what they are – what they enable and what they deny. They are pieces of the Whole – truth partially grasped. They are 'the bits of God that we see', the starting places for the journey into the mystery of God.

The cross is God's gift of a meeting place and what will come out of it 'has not yet been revealed'. God is keeping a secret and it is a secret for the whole world not just for the Church. We are seeking the signs of God's suffering, dying and rising in all that he has made. And here our search must leave behind its familiar language and pathways. If we like our religion well ordered, clearly defined and leaving us 'knowing where we are', then the cross of Christ is not the place for us. Some talk of Christianity like that, but it is not the faith we learn from Jesus. It is very doubtful how 'secure' the first disciples ever felt with him. He was so unpredictable. He didn't act like everyone else. They never knew what he was up to or where he was going next. And his teachings about life turned so much upside-down. After one very tough sermon on the cost of discipleship it is recorded that a number of his followers left him. In a moving and painful scene he turns to his closest disciples: 'You do not want to leave too, do you?' he asked. Peter's reply is honest and painful. He speaks for all who struggle to stay faithful to truth that is also painful. 'Lord, to whom shall we go? You have the words of eternal life. We believe and know that you are the Holy One of God' (John 6:67–9).

And that is where this book began – with an urge to break through the dullness of over-familiarity, and the struggle to try to 'tame' the way of Christ in order to live more comfortably with it. It is a search for more honest faith, stepping off treadmills of devotion that owe more to duty and vague guilt, than to hunger and the fire of the Spirit. It is a longing to draw near the real cross – rough, bloody and unfinished. A searching for the face of the one who died there . . . for a present reality.

2

Strange Fruit

Soon after moving in to my present home I spent a day trying to clear a very overgrown garden. I hacked my way through the undergrowth beside the road and built up a very satisfying bonfire. I worked with manic intensity, pouring with sweat and lost to the world. Then something made me look up. Through streaming eyes I noticed the faint outline of a man standing in thick smoke near the fence. He was from the local council. My fire was too big. The smoke was so thick it was slowing the traffic down. Cars were using their headlamps. It was very embarrassing. I couldn't even see my own house! I had been completely oblivious to the impact I was making on the world around me.

'The last thing we realise about ourselves is our effect,' reflects Hope Clearwater in *Brazzaville Beach*. In William Boyd's brilliant novel she sits in her beach hut and ponders the strange patterns of cause and effect, chaos and order in her life. Two other statements recur like a refrain. The first, with which the book begins and ends, is a statement by Socrates – 'The unexamined life is not worth living'. The second concerns our response to the daily uncertainties of life – 'What cannot be avoided must be welcomed'.[1]

Those convictions run right through this book too. They have in common an implicit admission of our dependency –

a call to careful and humble living. We are part of something much bigger than ourselves. We are not really in control and the most difficult task of all is to know ourselves as others know us – for better or for worse.

Divine necessity

Perhaps the hardest thing to accept when we look at the cross and the dying of Jesus is that it was really so necessary. Were things really so bad? Did it really need something so costly and destructive? Isn't it all rather exaggerated? Rather than face the awful implication of 'our effect' in this world, we hide behind vague and sentimental statements, 'The cross shows us how much God loves us' . . . It is much tougher than that.

> Every time we look at the cross Christ seems to say to us, 'I am here because of you. It is your sin I am bearing, your curse I am suffering, your debt I am paying, your death I am dying'. Nothing in history or in the universe cuts us down to size like the cross. All of us have inflated views of ourselves, especially in self-righteousness, until we have visited a place called Calvary. It is there, at the foot of the cross, that we shrink to our true size.[2]

The gospel records are very clear that the death of Jesus, as an innocent young man, was not the tragic cutting short of a life, an accident or disaster – but the fulfilment of his mission on earth. Jesus came to give his life for this world.

It was a self-giving of enormous costliness. As the time for his suffering and death approached Jesus agonised over what was ahead,

> 'Now my heart is troubled, and what shall I say? "Father save me from this hour"? No, it was for this very reason I came to this hour. Father, glorify your name.'

Then a voice came from heaven, 'I have glorified it, and
will glorify it again' . . . Jesus said, 'This voice was for your
benefit, not mine. Now is the time for judgment on this
world; now the prince of this world will be driven out. But
I, when I am lifted up from the earth, will draw all men to
myself.' He said this to show the kind of death he was going
to die. (John 12:27–8, 30–3)

So we are left with the question 'why' – and what must
our response be? If we cannot avoid the question, let us
welcome it. The way of the cross is not a way we would
ever have thought of or chosen. There is nothing 'natural'
about it. It is not the way the wise in this world would have
planned it (1 Cor. 1). No government would have proposed
it as a solution. No parliament would have seriously debated
it. Nor, in one sense, should the Christian Church ever
preach and teach the cross as if it is 'logical and sensible'. It
is not. What is more, we need to remember that this is a
message that was so disturbing and painful for the generation
of Jesus to hear that they did all they could to destroy him
utterly and with unspeakable violence. Worse still, it was the
sincerely religious people that led the attack. Dare we assume
that this same message is any less disturbing and unpalatable
today? Is there any less violence in us? Does our own religious
faith have any less capacity to deceive us? The late Dr Frank
Lake used to say, 'The truth is that we are at one and the
same time the beloved of God and the murderers of God'.
The cross remains a scandal and a stumbling block – as much
today as it was in the beginning (1 Cor. 1:23).

Pictures of salvation

'It was strange fruit, hanging on the tree', sang Billy Holli-
day. Travelling to a concert in a southern state of America,
the great blues singer had passed the victim of a lynch mob.

There is strange fruit to be found on the tree of Calvary also. Who would look in such a place for a message of world salvation?

When the New Testament writers looked for ways to understand and express what God had done through the cross of Christ they began with pictures from the world around them. Each was just a fragment. 'It is like this . . . but it is much more than this'. Underlying it all was the conviction that not only was the world broken, disordered and in revolt from God, it was also under judgement and facing terrible consequences for its ways. And to such a world God came, and comes, in Christ.

The victim on the altar

The first picture comes from the worship and theology of the Jewish temple. It is quite uncompromising. The world is in a state of sin, which each of us shares in. Wrongdoing has a consequence. Sin is the turning away from God. The consequence of sin is separation and death. In this world we are both sinners and sinned against but all are trapped in a deadly estrangement.

God is holy and pure. By his very nature he cannot abide sin. What is imperfect cannot endure what is perfect. This is the wrath of God. How can a sinful world endure the embrace of God without its destruction? It is the meeting of absolute opposites.

For such a world, God himself provides the sacrifice – and it is his own self in Christ. 'God made him who had no sin to be sin for us' (2 Cor. 5:21). When Christ suffered and died he had no sin of his own to pay for. He became the perfect offering for the sin of the world. 'Only innocence expiates,' wrote Simone Weil, 'crime suffers in quite a different way.' The consequence of this atoning sacrifice is that the barrier between God and his world is removed. Using the language of temple worship and ritual, the letter to the Hebrews says that now

> we have confidence to enter the Most Holy Place by the blood of Jesus, by a new and living way opened for us through the curtain, that is, his body, and since we have a great priest over the house of God let us draw near to God with a sincere heart in full assurance of faith, having our hearts sprinkled to cleanse us from a guilty conscience and having our bodies washed with pure water. (Heb. 10:19–22)

Prisoner at the bar

The second picture comes from the secular law courts. In the dock, humanity faces charges against which there is no plea but guilty. The sentence is passed and is carried out, not on the world, but on Christ. He died for us. But this is more than a picture of forgiveness. It is a picture of justification. We are now regarded as 'put right'. We have no more need to plead our guilt except to testify that Christ has taken the punishment and we are acquitted. And 'since we have been justified through faith, we have peace with God' (Rom. 5:1). We have been given life – not the old one back, but the life of Christ himself in exchange for ours. A Christian is one who has accepted this exchange in gratitude and trust. By faith, he or she is 'justified' by Christ. So, says Paul, 'I have been crucified with Christ and I no longer live, but Christ lives in me' (Gal. 2:20).

What am I bid?

The third picture comes from the market place – of commercial payment and debt. It is not so long ago in Western countries that men or women would be held in jail if they fell into debt. They waited there until someone paid a price for their freedom. The technical word for such a benefactor was a redeemer. A ransom was paid.

To a world morally and spiritually in debt for its actions and unable to pay, Christ comes and pays the price with his own life. Nor is it an act of magnificent power – but of great humility: 'The Son of Man did not come to be served, but to serve, and to give his life as a ransom for many' (Matt. 20:28). We are liberated by his gift. Set free. It is a price in complete excess of what we can ever be worth.

There is a strange fiction that we all collude with when it comes to the value we place on things. What makes an oil painting worth £30 million for example – particularly since the artist died penniless and unknown? What makes the suffering of one country worth fighting for while another is ignored? Who sets the value of our homes and our possessions?

The truth is that something is only as valuable as the price someone is willing to pay for it. What is true for our possessions is even more true for human life. If no one sees us as valuable in any sense we remain alone. If no one is willing to pay the ransom, the prisoner stays in jail. If no one is willing to pay for my spiritual and moral release I remain trapped in debt. 'For you know that it was not with perishable things . . . that you were redeemed . . . but with the precious blood of Christ' (1 Pet. 1:18–19).

A further question

It is surely not surprising that when the first Christians looked for ways to understand the cross and the story of salvation they should have borrowed many of their pictures from Roman judicial, legal and social life. It was an ordered, confident and 'just' system. It provided a useful backdrop to understanding the justice and righteousness of God's saving acts. It still does. Christianity, as it developed in Western Europe, has always had a fondness for these legal metaphors. My memory of studying 'Theories of the Atonement' as a theology student is of the overwhelming weight of legal and commercial metaphors. It was dull and very cerebral.

I would not have made a good lawyer. I don't think logically or in a linear fashion. I have an instinctive suspicion of any systematised way of understanding, let alone that of Christian faith. Once these pictures are removed from their living context they become abstracted 'theories'. Something in all this legal language feels sterile, detached and impersonal. The cross of Christ is none of these. Nor is God like the blindfolded figure of Justice above the Old Bailey – sword in one hand and scales in the other. It is wrong to see the cross as a coldly impartial and 'reasonable' approach to justice and human sin. It is not.

Even St Paul, a highly trained lawyer, is horrified by the thought that he might ever render his message (and himself!) respectable but ineffective. Christ sent him, he says, 'to preach the gospel – not with words of human wisdom, lest the cross of Christ be emptied of its power' (1 Cor. 1:17). So, he continues,

> When I came to you, brothers, I did not come with eloquence or superior wisdom as I proclaimed to you the testimony about God. For I resolved to know nothing while I was with you except Jesus Christ and him crucified. I came to you in weakness and fear, and with much trembling. My message and my preaching were not with wise and persuasive words but with a demonstration of the Spirit's power so that your faith might not rest on men's wisdom but on God's power. (1 Cor. 2:1–5)

A further question troubles me. What if Christ had lived and died in modern Beirut or in the refugee famine camps of the Sudan today? What if he had been crucified in Beirut or in the chaos of Amin's Uganda? What 'theories of the atonement' would his followers have used to teach his gift there?

The cross of Christ is a sign for all times and in all places. It is a sign of the *presence of Christ* in all times and places. There is a sense in which every generation seeks the place where its own joys and pains are met by the joy and the pain of God. And setting aside our over-tidy theological 'formulas' of the atonement, the cross tells us that it is a search that God has long since begun.

Then came light

Geoffrey Studdart Kennedy was an army chaplain in the First World War. He struggled with the meaning and relevance of the cross of Christ in an age suffering terrible violence.

> On June 7th, 1917, I was running to our lines half mad with fright, though running in the right direction, thank God, through what had been once a wooded copse. It was being heavily shelled. As I ran I stumbled and fell over something. I stopped to see what it was. It was an undersized, underfed German boy with a wound in his stomach and a hole in his head. I remember muttering, 'You poor little devil, what had you got to do with it? Not much great blonde Prussian about you.' Then came light. It may have been pure imagination, but that does not mean that it was not also reality, for what is called imagination is often the road to reality. It seemed to me that the boy disappeared and in his place there lay the Christ upon his cross, and cried, 'inasmuch as ye have done it unto the least of these my little ones ye have done it unto me.' From that moment on I never saw a battlefield as anything but a crucifix. From that moment on I have never seen the world as anything but a crucifix.[3]

3

Easter Was Late This Year

The Christian faith is cross shaped.

All religions have symbols or pictures by which they are recognised. Islam has the crescent moon. Buddhism is represented by an open lotus flower. Judaism has the Star of David. But the sign for Christian faith is the cross. How came the followers of a way of love and peace to adopt a logo of such appalling barbarity?

This is not such a strange question. It seems it was not until two hundred years after the death of Jesus that the Christian Church began openly to depict the cross in its art. There were good reasons for this. It was such a shameful and brutal death that it was unmentionable in public. Anyone dying such a death was stripped of any last shred of dignity or social respect. In the Jewish community they were held to be spiritually cursed as well. It was the death of the lowest criminals. It is hard to find a modern equivalent to the cross in terms of the immediate revulsion, disgust and terrible shame it evoked.

The first Christians often used alternative symbols such as a fish or dove. During times of persecution when Christian faith was not something to disclose to strangers it is known that a believer would trace half a fish shape in the dust with his or her foot. A fellow Christian would complete the shape.

Sign of shame

Who would look at a figure on a gallows as a source of religious truth and life? Who would take such a claim seriously? Yet within weeks of his death a religious 'sect' was worshipping a crucified man. They glorified in him and his dying. They celebrated his death as a 'victory'. They worshipped him as God from God. They claimed that through his death a new Kingdom was now beginning that would change the world. Nothing was untouched by it. Human nature and sinfulness were offered forgiveness and a new beginning. A new relationship with God was possible. World rulers were called to account and judged, while the poor and oppressed had special place in a new society of justice and peace.

This is the faith that the Jews found a blasphemous 'stumbling block' and the Greeks, plain madness (1 Cor. 1:23).

No one can come lightly to such a sign as the cross of Christ. If the man on this cross was really God then the world is faced with awful, terrible truths about itself. This is an event that must challenge and shatter every conviction we hold about ourselves.

But if this man on the cross is really divine then the world is faced with extraordinary truths about God. The testimony of the first Christians was that this same cross was a place of unimaginable mercy and a glorious gift to those who came near. 'To those who are perishing', says Paul, 'the message of the cross is foolishness . . . but to us who are being saved it is the power of God' (1 Cor. 1:18).

It remains a tough, uncompromising event to put at the centre of anyone's life and faith. It shouldn't surprise us that the first Christians struggled with the sign of the cross of

Jesus. There was a constant temptation to look for something less demanding – and there still is today. St Paul had to write to Christians who had so recently discovered the love of God through the cross:

> I am astonished that you are so quickly deserting the one who called you by the grace of Christ and are turning to a different gospel – which is really no gospel at all . . . May I never boast except in the cross of our Lord Jesus Christ, through which the world has been crucified to me, and I to the world.
>
> (Gal. 1:6 and 6:14)

Terribly familiar

I always leave a little pink
around the edges of my crosses
I cannot bear unbeauty

I honestly don't know why Jesus did it!
I can hardly accept *why he did it*.
The *why he did it* makes me feel guilty
about the pink around the edges.
During Lent, at least, I'd like to let the pink go.
I'd like to be content for forty days
with a cross that isn't pretty.
But . . . it is hard not to cheat a little
and search for soft, easy, pretty crosses.

O God of Lent remember me!
Help me take the fragile vessel that I am
and fill it with your dying.
Oh, for one short season at least
let me give up my pink-shadowed crosses,
my jewel-filled crosses,
my plastic crosses.
Take all clutter

> I decorate my crosses with,
> all the ways I camouflage
> your death and dying
> O God of Lent remember me![1]

No one should come lightly to the cross of Christ – but we do. Unlike the first Christians we live with the cross constantly. It is hard to avoid it. How many times a day do we pass crosses on churches, public buildings, monuments or in shops? In countries with a Christian culture, every city, town or village is full of crosses of all shapes and sizes.

The first Christians, struggling between awe and horror at what God had done in that place of shame, would never understand how familiar the cross has become to us. How can we gaze on it without awe, speak of it without pain and name it without worship? How did this sign of barbaric, terrible death become a popular piece of jewellery? Though we would probably not wear a miniature gallows or electric chair round our necks – that would be bad taste – we will wear a cross. Take up your cross? But which one? – there are so many to choose from.

We have lived with the cross for so long that it no longer disturbs us. We don't hear the questions it asks us. We dare not contemplate the death we see there. So we keep our crosses smooth and polished. We choose our crosses carefully because we don't want to shock or upset. They are respectable, dignified crosses. They don't embarrass us. They are shiny and stainless. We are ennobled in our reverencing of them. If there was any suffering and blood, it has been cleaned up. 'It is finished.'

Privatised faith

The Lee Abbey community in North Devon has a particularly dramatic way of celebrating Easter. On Good Friday three large crosses are carried in procession onto a hilltop overlooking the estate and a vigil is kept. I worked for several years in that community and those Good Friday vigils were deeply moving. But one year I will always remember. There on the hill an incident took place that changed my understanding of what we were doing. It disturbed me and when I tried to write it down I had to give the narrator a 'respectable' voice:

Easter was late this year
and Good Friday was a lovely warm spring day.
The meadows were bright with new colour, the winds
    fresh
and below the cliffs the Bristol channel
chopped and swelled a brilliant blue.
Exmoor is particularly beautiful in April.

On top of the headland (as we do each Easter)
we set three crosses, and there on the grass around
our Calvary, we sat and silently
remembered it all.

We hadn't been there long before we were noticed
from the road below. A car stopped and a family (not
    knowing
the estate was private) decided to join us for lunch,
climbing the hill with large picnic baskets and
noisy enthusiasm.

They found a spot to sit – just to the left of the
crosses.
And there they laughed and chattered and ate
their sandwiches apparently untouched by anything around
    them.
One of our group could finally stand it no more and went
and asked them to be quiet.

Lord I was so angry with them. Angry at being disturbed,
our prayers interrupted. Angry that the cross of Jesus
was being ignored, at their insensitivity; for having a
picnic on the hill of Calvary! As if the cross of Jesus
was a Bank Holiday entertainment all those years ago,
a sideshow for a holiday crowd – indifferent, laughing,
or looking for a place to eat lunch.

Jesus, remember me in your Kingdom,
With all who have made your cross respectable
and beautiful. With all who have privatised it
for our own devotions.

Jesus, remember me
with all who can look on your cross and ask no questions,
feel no shame. With all who can sit by your cross
and finish their lunch.
Remember me.

'We have privatised the cross' – that was sudden awareness.
This dying for all the world had become a personal, special
devotion. No one should disturb it. In my shame I tried to
look beyond this Easter of my own making and it suddenly
became just what it should be – an event of such awful dread,
wonder and holy mystery that I hardly dared draw near.

Remember me

When they came to the place called the Skull, there they
crucified him, along with the criminals – one on his right the
other on his left.

(Luke 23:33)

This is a powerful picture to meditate on. Christ, his arms
opened wide for us on the cross, and the two thieves on

either side. In Christian art, one thief is painted facing Christ and the other with his head turned away. Christ is facing the penitent thief. I wonder if it was as simple as that.

In fact both these criminals talk to Jesus. We know nothing of their lives and their crimes but one has apparently accepted his fate and even the justice of the sentence. The other is bitter and angry. Both make requests of Jesus. Both ask for salvation.

The penitent thief, with moving humility, says to Jesus, 'Remember me in your kingdom'. The other cries out in anger and pain at their situation, 'Aren't you the Christ? Save yourself and us!'

On those brutal bloody crosses, what is the real difference between the two prayers, uttered on either side of the out-stretched hands of Christ? It may be well not to divide these two responses too neatly into right and wrong. They are very human, and either way may be our own prayers in pain and crisis.

In particular, not all submission is more godly or spiritual than angry protest. The violent, abusive demand of the second criminal, in his extremis and bitterness may at least make us handle more carefully the places of anger and resentment in us, lest at the last, we find our hearts hardened by them.

It was 'while we were still helpless' that Christ died for us, sinners (Rom. 5:6). The cross of Jesus is a gift of divine love to people who have no way of receiving it. More than that, God's love is given to those who violently reject it. It is not that God doesn't hold us to account. There is a terrible price to pay for the wrong of this world. But there at the place of judgement we find open arms.

Nowhere is this welcome more needed than for those whose experience of life has proved too great to bear – for whom the cost of living and loving has been overwhelming and heart-breaking.

The hardest cross

I remember a man called Stan, a craftsman, whom I would like to call a friend. In 1984 there were many reunions and anniversary events across Europe to commemorate key battles that led to the end of the Second World War. Stan had taken part in the Normandy landings and the battle at Arnhem – the 'Bridge Too Far'.

When the anniversaries were over, in the autumn of that year, he set his affairs in order and, one day, took his own life. He was a private and sensitive man and we subsequently discovered that he had been one of the first soldiers to enter the concentration camps after the war. Although he never professed Christian faith in any public way he was, in his own fashion, a thoughtful and spiritual man. His passing was a terrible tragedy. Who can ever be sure that we have understood another's burden as they have known it? But in a personal attempt to reflect on his living and dying and experience of good and evil, I put words to paper.

> Lord
> have mercy on a man whose
> hardest cross
>   (we only glimpsed)
> was caring much
>
> who all these days looked out
> through the private scars
> of wounded sight
> have mercy on a weary heart
>   (and haunted too we think)
> until remembering
> itself became a shadow that
> now cast across his face
> his world and

into all to come
                    (he thought)

have mercy
for whether yet he knew your name
his hands knew well
and loved
the texture of your mind

Lord have mercy on a man
whose last work
chosen designed completed alone
was his own life

and that
he gave to you

Into eternity

We too must come to the place called the Skull. We have a journey to make. It may be a journey away from indifference, carelessness. It may be a journey through the dullness of sheer overfamiliarity with religious words and signs. For some it will be a painful journey from despair and death. Wherever we come from, with protest or longing, we find that God has already journeyed long and painfully towards us.

This is a journey into our beginnings – our beginnings in divine love, without hatred or rejection. For the cross is an action not a statement, a real dying, not a philosophical parable. 'God was in Christ reconciling the world to himself' (Col. 1:20).

This is a journey into eternity, into the mystery of an unimaginable gift.

4

Standing in the Breach

What do you see in the engraving on the next page? Since I first came across it some years ago it has always moved me. It illustrates the most important gift of the cross in the New Testament – the gift of reconciliation. It is a picture of restored relationships, of the meeting of opposites and of divided things. The artist, Scilla Verney, was working on this engraving when she died of cancer.[1]

The broken whole

There are two fractured pieces being awkwardly and painfully held together by the figure of Christ. It speaks to me of the cross as a place of new meeting – not of friends – but of separated, alienated worlds. The terse angles of his twisted body accentuate the costliness of this. His arms are stretched wide, reaching deeply into the broken sides beside him. The two pieces would not naturally fit together without him. They are held together through and in him.

This is a picture of reconciling, of standing between and enabling a meeting to happen. All Christian living, and all of this book, is the search to enter the truth this engraving reveals. It forms a visual aid for this chapter.

For the New Testament believers this reconciling happened at many different levels. No part of life was untouched by it. This vision of the meeting and unifying of all things in God was also recorded as something that has objectively happened. God had done something through Christ on the cross. The basis of reconciliation was complete. In Christ all things now hold together. The goal of our life and prayer and journey of faith is to enter and realise the truth of what has already been achieved.

It is a vision that expands with the telling, but it can be summarised on three levels – personal, social and cosmic.

Coming home

On a lonely track, in the middle of the night, a man stood in despair. He had been a wanderer for years. While it was fashionable he had lived as a hippy wherever he could find shelter and drugs. In India he had been living with a couple where for the first time he had had some sense of home and security. Earlier that evening they had told him they were splitting up. Peter felt as if he had nothing left to live for. Finally, under the stars of the wide Indian sky he called out, 'God, if you're there, help me!' And there in the silence someone answered him, deep within him.

As he told of this beginning to his conversion to Christian faith, Peter's voice and bearing expressed the depth of this personal, life-changing meeting with God. He now realised that this was what his whole life had been a searching for – the longing to cross the divide between himself and the God who made him. It is the oldest, most terrible divide of all.

In Scilla Verney's engraving, Christ fills the gap, hangs in the breach beween God and our world. Through the cross the ancient separation between God and humanity has been overcome. We enter a new relationship with our Creator. St Paul says, 'If, when we were God's enemies, we were reconciled to him through the death of his Son, how much more, having been reconciled, shall we be saved through his life! Not only is this so, but we also rejoice in God through our Lord Jesus Christ, through whom we have now received reconciliation' (Rom. 5:10–11). In another place he expresses this even more emphatically, 'If anyone is in Christ he is a new creation; the old has gone, the new has come! All this is from God, who reconciled us to himself through Christ . . . ' (2 Cor. 5:17–18).

Through Christ, we may enter a new relationship with God. He calls us his children, sons and daughters. We call him 'Abba', 'Father'. We meet together in Christ. St Paul describes this as an adoption. Borrowing the language of Roman law whereby a child became legally part of a new family, St Paul expects the Holy Spirit to awaken in us the reality of our new status.

> Those of you who are led by the Spirit of God are sons of God. For you did not receive a spirit that makes you a slave again to fear, but you received the Spirit of sonship. And by him we cry, 'Abba, Father'. The Spirit himself testifies with our spirit that we are God's children. Now if we are children, then we are heirs – heirs of God and co-heirs with Christ . . . (Rom. 8:14–17)

The final prayer at the end of the Communion service says it simply and beautifully: 'Father of all, we give you thanks and praise, that when we were still far off you met us in your Son and *brought us home* . . . '[2]

A new society

Lives open to God are opened in a new way to each other. There is a social and international dimension to this reconciliation. In fact St John says that unless this is true, our love for God is highly suspect (1 John 4:7). There is no such thing as private belief in the Bible. In Ephesians chapter 2 it is through the blood of Christ on the cross that separated peoples and cultures are reunited – to God and to each other.

> His purpose was to create in himself one new man out of the two and in this one body to reconcile both of them to God through the cross. He came and preached peace to you who were far away and peace to those who were near. For through him we both have access to the Father by one Spirit.
>
> (Eph. 2:15–18)

In Cape Town, South Africa, there is a multi-racial community called 'the Community of the Broken Wall'. It takes its name from the words of St Paul when he said of Christ, 'He himself is our peace who has made the two one and has destroyed the barrier, the dividing wall of hostility . . . ' (Eph. 2:14).

It could be the name of every Christian community and congregation.

A new cosmos

There is a cosmic dimension to the reconciling work of Christ. This is perhaps the hardest aspect to grasp but it must be acknowledged. We read of Christ that 'God was pleased to have all his fulness dwell in him, and through him to reconcile to himself all things, whether things on earth or things in heaven, by making peace through his blood, shed on the cross' (Col. 1:19–20). Later in the letter Christ is described as having 'disarmed the powers and authorities', making 'a public spectacle of them, triumphing over them by the cross' (2:15).

In the dying of Christ on the cross the whole ordering of the cosmos is shaken. Jesus himself prophesied this, 'Now is the time for judgement on this world; now the prince of this world will be driven out' (John 12:31). Through the cross the power of evil is broken. Principalities and powers must now acknowledge a greater Lord. Even so, the dimension of spiritual warfare and evil is not one to enter into with any easy triumphalism. For most of us the struggle to submit our lives and wills to Christ is warfare enough. But many who prayed for the recent Gulf war became aware of more than just their own fears and the cost of human violence. They also knew the dead weight of spiritual oppression that attended the onset of the conflict. The people of the cross will share in the conflict at the heart of the cross.

Divine absence

The cross challenges our understanding of power. In our uncertain and fearful world it is tempting to look for a God who is more powerful than the powers we fear. But if we speak of the victory of the cross of Christ we have to ask ourselves what kind of power is at work there?

Here a second feature of Scilla Verney's engraving is reveal-ing. Christ is actually defined by his absence. He is seen only in what he brings together. This is the Christ who set aside the glory and 'presence' that is his by right. Though rich in glory he became poor among us. He emptied himself. The one who could command all things 'became obedient'. He was willing to set aside ultimate power, willing finally to enter the death of his own creation.

This, we have already noted, is the way God loves. This is divine love. The technical term for this self-emptying is 'kenosis' (from Phil. 2). It characterises all God's ways with us. And it confronts us with a new way of love – and a radically new understanding of power. This is a God who does not command from above, imposing his structure and order and strength. Jesus explicitly rejects the earthly model of authority. 'You know that the rulers of the Gentiles lord it over them, and their high officials exercise authority over them. Not so with you.' Their model is Christ who came 'to serve, and to give his life as a ransom for many' (Matt. 20:25 and 28).

He is a God who comes to us from beneath. He enters our world through its weakness, its wounds, its places of rejection. He shares our emptiness. He enters the absence of all we long for and becomes it. He makes it his own. He enters our desolation so completely that he makes our deepest cry his own, 'My God, why have you forsaken me?'

No love is so longed for. Yet the truth is that no love is so instinctively resisted. At the cross we have to face the question: 'Is this the God I want or do I look for another?'

No other way

On 15 January 1991 the United Nations' deadline requiring Iraq to withdraw from Kuwait expired. Shortly afterwards the war began. Many churches stayed open that day and arranged special times of prayer for peace. In one such service I knelt, struggling for words, for guidance, for any glimmer that what we were offering was of use to God or the world. Many felt overwhelmed by a sense of helplessness at that time.

A mental picture persisted in my mind. I saw two rows of tanks facing each other across a narrow strip of desert. Between them walked a man in a dusty robe carrying a cross. It was a strange picture. The figure of Christ looked oddly old-fashioned and hopelessly out of place surrounded by impassive military power. There was no sense of authority about him. He offered no 'answers'.

I thought long on this picture and increasingly sensed the loneliness of Christ. I felt embarrassed by him walking there. I felt the folly of the cross. I wanted another way – a way of power. I wanted a presence, not an absence. I wanted – finally admitting it – a God I could be proud of. I wanted a

God whose power and authority I could point to and respect. What do we do with the apparent absence of God in so much of the world? What kind of God is this crucified One? Is there no other way? Like the thief on the cross we want to shout, 'Aren't you God!? *Do* something – and help us while you are at it!'

Praying was a painful experience that day. As I wrestled with anger and helplessness and the 'absence' of God I began to realise how deeply I was part of the conflict itself. I really wanted to be able to line up a longer row of bigger tanks with 'GOD' written over the top. A display of ultimate power to cow and crush the ways of evil. At another level I wanted a divine parent, who in the dark night of this world would hear our cries, come in, turn on the light and 'make it all right'.

Is this man at Calvary the God we want? The cross of Christ is the way of divine weakness and vulnerability. It challenges all our ideas of power and influence. This is a God who refuses to 'take over' our lives but comes alongside and shares them. And the cross tells us that in our fury we reject such a God. In a deadly refusal to 'grow up' we go looking elsewhere for something else to take us over and make us feel secure.

Christ on the cross draws all this out – all the insecurity, all the deadly dependency, all that we refuse to face about ourselves. There God takes all the dark brooding evil this angry, broken world can throw at him. It all seems to be drawn to a climax at the cross. In one moment of time, darkness over the whole land, the human heart spends itself, out of an abyss of terrible despair – an orgy of earthly and cosmic violence, an agonising kenosis.

And Christ accepts it all. He pours himself into the abyss in return. He descends into hell with the presence of divine love. His arms are still open.

The justification of God

We may find much Christian belief rather strange. We may feel the same about those who go to church! Christian rituals and practices may be profoundly irritating. But we need to recognise that our real struggle is with Christ. Does that sound too obvious? Christianity is Christ. It is to him that we must bring our questions, make our pleas or hurl our denunciations. In a profound sense the cross is not simply the justification of a sinful world. It is the justification of God.

For the first time in my life I dared to demand an explanation. When none came, I was angrier than I ever remember being. I turned my eyes on the plain wooden cross and I remembered Calvary. I stood in the crowd which crucified him, hating and despising him. With my own hands I drove the nails into his hands and his feet, and with bursting energy I flogged him and reviled him and spat with nauseated loathing. Now *he* should know what it felt like – to live in the creation he had made. Every breath brought from me the words: 'Now you know! Now you know!'

And then I saw something which made my heart stand still. I saw his face, and on it twisted every familiar agony of my own soul. 'Now you know' became a whisper as I, motionless, watched his agony. 'Yes, now I know' was the passionate and pain-filled reply. 'Why else should I come?' Stunned, I watched his eyes search desperately for the tiniest flicker of love in mine, and as we faced one another in the bleak and the cold, forsaken by God, frightened and derelict, we loved one another and our pain became silent in the calm.

Nothing can bind us closer than common dereliction for nowhere else is companionship so longed for. From that moment I was tied on to Christ, knowing the rope would hold if I fell in the climb as he led me slowly and firmly out of hell, sometimes out of sight ahead of me, then dear and firm and calm as I scrambled up to his side.[3]

PART B

This Is My Body

'freed us from the slavery of sin'

5

Love Fore-given

Two other men, both criminals, were also led out with him to be executed. When they came to the place called the Skull, there they crucified him, along with the criminals – one on his right, the other on his left. Jesus said, 'Father, forgive them, for they do not know what they are doing.'

(Luke 23:32–4)

In 1979, a revolution toppled the brutal dictatorship of President Somoza in Nicaragua. A new government was formed and Thomas Borge was appointed Minister for the Interior. He was a committed Christian who had suffered torture at the hands of Somoza's secret police. His wife had been raped and killed by them.

As part of his new responsibilities he visited the jails where the former members of the police force were being held pending trial. He reached one cell where he recognised two of the men. 'Do you recognise me?' he asked them. 'I am Borge whom you tortured and whose wife your colleagues raped and murdered.' They couldn't look at him.

'Well you are going to feel the full force of this revolution', he said. 'I forgive you. Go, you are free.'[1]

Writing in the sand

There must always be a sense of scandal about real forgiveness. What does such a story leave you feeling? It is moving and courageous. But doesn't a voice inside want to protest? 'Just a moment, he can't do that! Life isn't like that! That is taking forgiveness too far.'

What did the loved ones of Jesus feel at Golgotha, surrounded by abusive crowds, watching the nails being driven in, the brutality and injustice, then to hear Jesus say: 'Father, forgive them, for they know not what they do', and what do those words from the cross arouse in you and me?

Throughout his earthly ministry Jesus got into trouble for forgiving people. He claimed unique authority to forgive sins in this world. In doing so he was claiming to be God and he was condemned for blasphemy. But he also taught that everyone should forgive – and forgive endlessly (Matt. 18:21ff). Forgiveness, for Jesus, was not just something to do with being God. It said something profound about being truly human. The failure to forgive leaves us outside God's forgiveness and outside society. No belonging is possible without forgiveness. In all his preaching he taught that forgiving was the only way to live in God's blessing. It was radical and uncompromising. 'You have heard that it was said, "Love your neighbour and hate your enemy." But I tell you: Love your enemies and pray for those who persecute you' (Matt. 5:43–4). 'If you love only those who love you what credit is that to you? Even sinners love those who love them!' (Luke 6:32). 'If you forgive men when they sin against you, your heavenly Father will also forgive you. But if you do not forgive . . . ' (Matt. 6:14–15).

Few things made Jesus more angry than the pitiless condemnation of a sinner by *fellow sinners*. St John recorded an incident where a woman was dragged before Jesus having been caught in the very act of adultery. Her accusers demanded her stoning. They sought no condemnation for the man who had been with her. They felt no guilt at trapping her. Jesus wrote in the sand with his finger and then pronounced the judgement of God. 'If any one of you is without sin, let him be the first to throw a stone at her' (John 8:7–8). The church still remembers this story as 'The woman taken in adultery'. It is not. It is actually the story of the 'Men taken in hypocrisy'. There is a lesson in forgiveness here we have yet to learn.

The violence within

When the people of the cross speak of forgiveness they are not appealing to any natural reserves or 'better instincts'. If it were so natural would we not have found a way long ago? It is not the 'sensible thing to do' or the natural response of 'any reasonable person'.

At a safe distance from the most explicit evidence of our human capacity for cruelty and revenge we easily speak of forgiveness as a kind of moderation. We watch the news or read the papers and can't believe that people can do such things. 'If only they could love each other – just sit down and talk.' So from the comfort of our English homes, we watch the sectarian hatred in Northern Ireland and listen to politicians appealing for 'moderation'.

The violence lies within each of us though we are well practised at hiding from it much of the time. A few years ago I went to see the film *Gandhi*. This Indian holy man has always been a hero of mine. I was very moved by his non-violent philosophy (though my convictions have never been seriously tested!).

Early in the film there is a scene from South Africa where the young Gandhi is organising a protest against the recent Pass laws. Beside a small fire he makes a speech, grave and courteous, and then begins to burn his pass book and those of his friends. The police arrive and he is warned to stop.

He quietly goes on burning the books. The policeman strikes him once, twice. Gandhi continues, blood on his face. He is struck again and falls to the ground. With trembling hands he reaches for another pass book and puts it on the fire. The policeman looks at him, baffled and powerless.

As I watched that scene in the darkness of the cinema I suddenly realised with a hot sense of shame, that my overwhelming urge in that moment was to beat the policeman's head in. What is more I would have enjoyed it!

Revolution

The life of forgiveness is a total radical revolution. The capacity to forgive is a gift of grace: it comes from outside us. Indeed we are so blind to our own prejudices that without this grace we cannot see them for what they are.

The word of forgiveness breaks into our world and our lives and totally disarms us. It is tough and uncompromising. There is nothing sentimental about it. It is harder to forgive than to hate. Far from leading us immediately to life and joy it may often leave us wanting to throw up. 'Forgiveness', wrote Simon Tugwell, 'is not something for people with weak stomachs'.[2] Forgiving is not being 'nice' – it is being godly. Ultimately, it is a crucifying experience.

This leads us into one of the hardest aspects of forgiveness and reconciliation we learn from Christ. It is fore-given. It is offered in advance. It is not to be negotiated. It is love offered without guarantee of return or acceptance. Who wants to be that exposed? Who can bear that kind of vulnerability? How hard it is when you have let go of pride, screwed up your courage and gone to someone to say sorry or offer forgiveness and it is not received. How hard not to take it back again! But that is exactly the love of God in Christ who 'while we were still sinners . . . died for us' (Rom. 5:8). God fore-gave his love to a world that rejected it. We have noted the painful paradox already – that the cross reveals us, at one and the same time, to be the beloved of God and the murderers of God.

I have never forgotten the testimony of a missionary from the Middle East whose wife had been taken to hospital with acute back trouble. In the next bed was a Muslim woman whose husband somehow discovered their neighbours were Christian. The man was violently abusive and did everything possible to disturb their sleep and make life thoroughly uncomfortable. He even smoked cigarettes to give this back sufferer the agony of coughing fits. The missionary spoke of his turmoil inside. He was angry. He wanted to fight back. No reasonable appeals had made any difference. He wrestled with a Christian response. One night he took the man's shoes as he slept. He cleaned and polished them and put them back. In the morning he watched the man's face as he realised what had been done for him – a terrible struggle between anger and wonder, the struggle to receive Christ's love or refuse it.

The people of the cross are those who are bound to refuse all enemies by loving them. They cannot live with the barriers of prejudice or ignorance. They wrestle with the terrible depths of this world's divisions. Through the appalling costliness of Christ's love, they seek a new world.

'Father forgive'. What, everything? Everyone? Isn't this kind of forgiving unrealistic? Does it work? Isn't it immoral? Must I forgive everyone I have ever hated and left unloved; everyone who has ever hurt me? Are we to forgive every terrorist bomber, every cruel dictator, every Tiananmen Square, every child abuser, every rapist? Every selfish, bigoted, indifferent act on earth . . . all forgiven?

Burning coals

But forgiveness is not a passive acceptance. No one 'gets away with it' when words of forgiveness are spoken. Forgiving involves judgement. When forgiveness is offered or received there is a recognition of the need to change attitudes or actions. It involves acceptance and reconciliation. Following the way of forgiveness is profoundly costly. It shakes and re-evaluates things within us.

St Paul says forgiveness is like a fire. We still speak of it in this way. In the moment when a personal attitude or action is exposed for what it is we speak of 'burning with shame'. Forgiveness brings us under judgement. Forgiveness is a terrible and wonderful gift to give anyone. It burns us. And any relationship in which forgiveness is offered is changed forever. So, says St Paul,

> 'If your enemy is hungry, feed him;
> if he is thirsty, give him something to drink.
> In doing this, you will heap burning coals on his head.'
>
> (Rom. 12:20)

It seems that any act of mercy in this world leaves the person receiving it with the responsibility to live in the same way. The burning coals are not punishment. The fire of forgiveness, if received, frees the one receiving it to become a forgiver in return. It burns up the bitterness, the pride and stubbornness that refused love and made an enemy in the first place. Jesus tells the story of the employee whose large debt is written off by his employer but who goes straight out and refuses the same generosity to someone who owed *him* much less. This hardness of heart then earns the man a judgement that his initial debt never merited (Matt. 18:21–35).

Broken walls

But the demands of forgiving are found everywhere in life, not just among avowedly religious communities.

Since the demolition of the Berlin Wall and the reunification of Germany, reconciliation has been a key word as people have struggled to adapt to new societies and relationships. Memories and attitudes have been disturbed. In Britain a Cabinet minister resigned after remarks about the German people in the light of the Second World War. In the same year that Germany was reunified, the British Poppy Day appeal chose a poster campaign that deliberately evoked old fears, reminding people of how easily Britain might have been under German rule today.

For the East and West Germans themselves these sudden changes must have been traumatic. One group of East Germans has found the adjustment too hard to bear. Among the 85,000 Stasi, the secret police, there has been a high incidence of mental breakdown and suicide since the Berlin Wall came down. These men and women were highly trained and indoctrinated. In their world it was very clear who was good and who was bad. Real and ideological walls surrounded them and gave them the security of easily recognising friends and enemies. They knew their work and vocation on this earth with precision and clarity. And suddenly it had all changed. The walls were broken through. 'Friends' and 'enemies' were talking, shaking hands, smiling.

A friend in South Africa recently wrote of a similar crisis facing Christian leaders in the black townships. For so long they had been forced to take sides in the political conflicts. They had buried the victims of oppression and comforted their families. They had prayed for reconciliation and peace between the races. And suddenly there was a breakthrough. Nelson Mandela was released. Government and A.N.C. leaders met for talks. It was the change that they had worked and prayed for for so long. But in its advent Christians have found themselves facing a loss of identity and role. When you have been used to hammering on a wall of indifference and neglect for the whole of your life and that wall suddenly crumbles, what do you do with your fists? Forgiveness is more difficult than deciding someone is lovable after all. It shakes life up – both for people and for nations.

A little dying

By acting with regard to no one but himself, a man once brought another relationship to the point of collapse. When the incident came into the open the couple, and their friends, showed him remarkable love and publicly forgave him. When I met him he was a man in pain. 'I can't take all this forgiveness', he said, 'I'd rather someone hit me in the face!'

Just as something must die for forgiveness to be offered, so something must die for forgiveness to be received. Forgiving is a disturbing and fearful journey through our familiar barriers into – what? What do we expect to find on the other side of death?

When we receive the forgiveness of another
the depths of our personalities are disturbed.
For it means that the worst in us has been accepted,
and that means a kind of death. We have no need
to fight our own worst selves any more.
And it is hard to receive this truth. We turn against
our forgiver in self-justification. 'How dare you accept
me as I am and not condemn me!' So folk turned against
Christ for so accepting them. But God's forgiveness is
without condition. It sweeps us off our feet. We want
to make conditions so that there can be still a core
under our control. Let go completely.
This is death, but it is necessary if we are to find life
– to let go into God.[3]

6

This Side of Heaven

No love can be given or received where there is no acceptance. No offer of true forgiveness has, written between the
lines, 'OK, just once more . . . this is your last chance.'
Without acceptance no real change is possible. This is the
paradox: when I am loved for who I am, I am free to become
who I can be. This coming to acceptance, of ourselves or of
others, is as demanding and searching as forgiveness itself.

Human becomers

One model for understanding the development of human
personality and potential is called the Dynamic cycle.[1]

In an ideal world, where the stages of the cycle develop as
they should, human life begins with birth into an environ-
ment of unconditional, affirming and accepting love – of me
for who I am. Out of that acceptance comes a sense of being
sustained, a sense of well-being. This brings the strength to
explore life, to seek to achieve, to be motivated towards ideas
and people. That in turn leads to achievement, which in a
secondary but important way underlines the acceptance and
worth we began with. It is pictured thus:

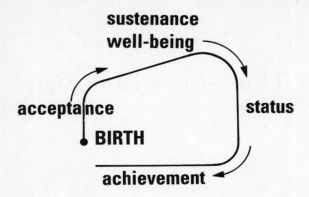

This describes the earthly life cycle of Jesus whose sense of worth throughout his life was in the knowledge of the Father's unconditional love and delight. But as someone once said, Jesus was the only truly human being – the rest of us are human *becomers*. The Dynamic cycle illustrates an ideal human experience. But for all of us life has been a flawed and wounding experience in varying measure. Above all, our experience of human love has been incomplete. We may hear the message 'I love you as you are' but life teaches us that underneath are unspoken conditions to that love – 'I will love you as you are *as long as* . . . '. That means that our subsequent sense of well-being and worth becomes part of our search for acceptance and love. Our achieving can become a way of earning our security in accepting love. In the brokenness of this world, all of us have experienced the receiving of love and also the need to earn it.

Looking back

Any who seek, through counselling and friendship, to
unravel the complex patterns of unmet longing and the
wounds of incomplete or absent love will come to an important point sooner or later: the place of acceptance. For example, the person who now begins to glimpse the real poverty
of a parent's love and opens up the deep pain and anger of
those early years can move no further and grow no more,
until there is a willingness and ability to accept. This is not
a condoning or an excusing. It is simply recognising that that
is the way things were and in human terms nothing will
change that actual experience from what it was.

Illustrating this from the experience of one of her clients,
psychotherapist Alice Miller makes the same point.

> It is one of the turning points in analysis when . . . the patient
> comes to the emotional insight that all the love he has captured
> with so much effort and self denial was not meant for him as
> he really was, that the admiration for his beauty and achieve-
> ments was aimed at the beauty and these achievements, not
> at the child himself. In analysis, the small and lonely child
> wakes up and asks: 'What would have happened if I had
> appeared before you, bad, ugly, angry, jealous, lazy, dirty,
> smelly? Where would your love have been then? And I was
> all these things as well. Does this mean that it was not really
> me whom you loved, but only what I pretended to be? The
> well-behaved, reliable, emphatic, understanding, and con-
> venient child, who in fact was never a child at all? What
> became of my childhood? Have I not been cheated out of it?
> I can never return to it. I can never make up for it. From the
> beginning I have been a little adult. My abilities – were they
> simply misused?'[2]

There is anger. There is grieving. This journey has all the
stages of actual bereavement. But from the place of accept-

ance comes the healing freedom to change, to grow – and the beginnings of forgiveness.

Accepting God

I asked the question in the last chapter, 'Is the God of the cross the God we want?' It is not a question to simply answer 'yes' or 'no' to. A friend of mine described his experience on retreat. He was given a verse of Scripture each day by a very discerning retreat conductor. He was enjoying the silence and felt prayer deepening. Then he was given the theme of 'Hope' and the verse from St Paul who prays, 'I keep asking that the God and Father of our Lord Jesus Christ, the glorious Father, may give you the Spirit of wisdom and revelation, so that you may know him better . . . that the eyes of your heart may be enlightened in order that you may know the hope to which he has called you' (Eph. 1:17–18). Hope. He meditated on the word – it had a fresh sense of 'possibility', 'openness'. Hope is a doorway into life, he reflected. Why not open it? And then it was as if doors deep inside him shook and trembled and voices from the depths in pain and fury cried, 'Don't open it! . . . Don't ask us to open up. We have been let down too often . . . it doesn't work . . . don't ask us to live with the pain.' They were powerful voices of anger and despair and with them surfaced a tearful litany of memories where life, received with vulnerable trusting openness, had let him down.

We have protected and hidden our wounds for so long that our defences are powerful against the invitation to change. We are suspicious. And rightly so. As Jean Vanier once wrote, 'people who have been much hurt have a right to know that they are loved'.

John Cleese, in his hilarious film *Clockwise*, expressed this another way, as only he can. As he contemplates the ruins of his life around him, lying by the side of a country road in a monk's habit he mutters, 'Despair . . . I can live with the despair, it's the hope I can't cope with'.

In the end our protest must be directed at God. After all, 'he made us and not we ourselves'. He is God. In this fallen world our experience of God is as incomplete as our experience of human love. It is unrealistic to suppose that we have never felt let down by God. His ways are often baffling in this world. Our pictures of him may be a complete distortion. Yet we persist in a desperate fiction that, as one Christian urged me in all sincerity, 'If things go wrong in life, we should never blame God'. The implication of that advice is that it is always our fault.

Because our identity and destiny are so deeply tied up in our understanding of God, the journey into believing and loving will be a far more ambivalent experience than we dare to admit. If we could see our depths we would find confused layers of belief and unbelief, of love and rejection. Something about the purity of divine love opens us to our best and to our worst. There will be conflict. The two sides meet on the cross of Christ.

Identikit of God

For some years I have enjoyed running a workshop called 'Identikit of God'. It works like this. On a sheet of paper are listed the main names for God in the Bible. On the other side are listed the main names we are given in relation to God.

Members of the group are then asked to go down each list and rate each name according to whether it means 'a lot', 'something', 'very little' to them. The golden rule is to be honest!

The results are always the same. From the names of God, people always choose 'Father' and 'Lord', first and second. Of their own names before God they overwhelmingly choose 'sinner' followed by 'child'. Low on the first list come such names as 'Saviour' and 'Friend'. Bottom of the second list come such self-confident affirmations as 'new man/woman'. 'Son/daughter' is only a little higher.

These results puzzle and disturb me. What relationship between God and his people is reflected here? It seems that although we call God 'Father' the knowledge of him leaves us feeling like inadequate and naughty children – sinners. Where is the realisation that in God's love we are called sons and daughters? This is not a picture of dependent, insecure children. It is a picture of young adults on the verge of coming of age, full of the promise and hope of life and preparing to enter an inheritance that is uniquely theirs in all eternity.

Forgiving heaven

But that is not where we are starting from. This wounded, fearful, distorted picture of our relating to God and he to us is where we must begin. This means acceptance. And God, who accepts us as we are, will start from there also. Rowan Williams once wrote, 'The cry to God as Father in the New Testament is not the calm acknowledgment of a universal truth about God's abstract "Fatherhood". It is a child's cry out of nightmare'.[3]

'Be reconciled to God', urged Paul (2 Cor. 5:20). And all of life is summed up in that task. It is rarely preached, though it is certainly true, that we will each need, in our own way, to come to a place where we *forgive God*. We seek a place where we can accept all our false images, the wounds of incomplete love, the wounds of rejection and absence. We must mourn them and with 'trembling hope' welcome the crucified love of God into those depths.

'Give me a candle of the Spirit, O God, as I go down into

the deeps of my being. Show me the hidden things, the creatures of my dreams, the storehouse of forgotten memories and hurts. Take me down to the spring of my life, and tell me my nature and my name. Give me freedom to grow, so that I may become that self, the seed of which you planted in me at my making. Out of the deeps I cry to you, O Lord'.

And perhaps to such an offering we dare to hear a response – 'Words of God?'? 'Forgive me for having created a world in which so much pain has to be allowed to happen if I am truly to be a God of love and enable you to love with a love that is worthy of the name . . . '[4]

Forgiving earth

We cannot be reconciled with heaven without being reconciled to earth. Indeed, as Neville Ward once put it, 'we must forgive earth for not being heaven'. This is particularly hard for the community of the church. We are so aware of the 'demands' of heaven that earth is an embarrassment. We can be so full of what we 'should' be and 'ought' to be, so aware of what we are not, that we cannot live with who we are. The community of the church can often be a place where people feel least accepted. We require special clothes, special behaviour, special songs, special language. We learn, without being told, that certain things can be talked about and others cannot. We may laugh and be 'strong', but tears and weakness cause embarrassment. We may believe strongly but not voice our doubts. So we all learn to be 'acceptable' – a community created in the image of its own unfaced anxieties. And so the very place that worships God for his love and forgiveness and unconditional acceptance becomes a place where we deny it to each other. 'The church is the only army to wound its own soldiers', said one battered Christian, feeling utterly rejected in his efforts to be honest in his needs.

Jesus constantly created social scandal through his willingness to ignore the respectable, institutional side of religion,
and to insist on meeting real people where they were. Those
who were hiding behind the façade of religious faith and the
illusion of its status and piety found his love coming from
behind and underneath them. The love of Jesus always comes
in at our beginnings, in at our depths. He comes to heal the
dynamic cycle of our lives at source.

I once heard the late Dr Frank Lake lecture on the Dynamic
Cycle model. He drew the cycle and spoke of the vital need
for human life to begin in accepting, unconditional love. He
spoke of the casualties in life for whom the effort of earning
and seeking ungiven love was too much. 'Now where is the
cross in all this?' he asked. Most of us produced a variation
of this drawing.

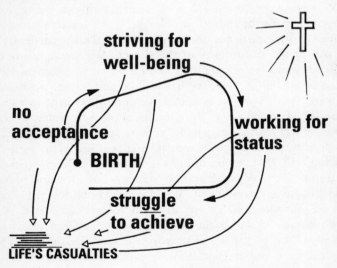

We drew the cross above, beyond, calling us to better life,
an example, a hope.

'No', he said, 'this is where the cross is.'

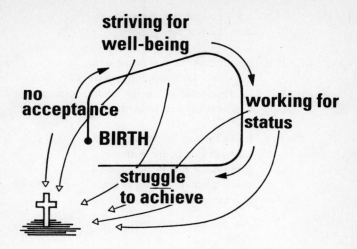

He drew it underneath it all, in the middle of the pile of life's casualties, the wounded, the hopeless, the rejected.

Out of despair

The community found at the cross of Christ is one that is slowly and painfully learning the way of trust out of rejection, of hope out of despair, of vulnerability out of self-protecting strength. It is a community of human becomers, learning, through the gift of God's vulnerable, accepting, suffering love, to risk the journey into reconciliation, forgiveness and life itself.

WE MUST FORGIVE EARTH FOR NOT BEING
HEAVEN

I forgive   earth for not being heaven
             time for not being eternity

faith for not being certainty
dust for not being glory

I forgive   beginnings for not being ends
            questions for not being answers
            confusion for not being understanding
            darkness for not being light

I forgive   mind for not being heart
            man for not being woman
            passion for not being love
            conflict for not being peace
            evil for not being good

            you for not being me

I forgive

and holding a mirror to the prayer
I start again

I forgive forgiveness never ending[5]

7

O Happy Fault!

The mime artist Marcel Marceau plays a character who comes across a box of masks. Every human mood and emotion are there and in front of a mirror he enjoys trying them on. He ends up with two favourite masks – happy and sad. He amuses himself by switching them faster and faster. But one mask suddenly sticks on his face and he can't get it off. He becomes increasingly desperate in his attempts to prize the mask off and all the while his face shows a wildly happy expression. The mime closes with the man wearing his broadly grinning face. But now his shoulders begin to shake and his hands cover his face and we sense the tears and terrible despair hidden behind the mask.

Behind the mask

Sin is really a distortion. We are made in God's likeness but we have learned to live with masks and caricatures. We have lost our real selves. In the book of Genesis we read that when Adam and Eve first disobeyed they hid from God and covered up from each other. But the ancient church doctrine of Original Sin is itself a distortion of the truth. For sin was never original in this world. What was original was God's goodness. 'God saw all that he had made, and it was very good' (Gen. 1:31). In emphasising Original Sin instead of Original Goodness we are still believing in the caricature we have become. The idea of original sin puts our distorted humanity at the centre of things rather than God's goodness. It is small wonder that many people struggle to move beyond the sense of their sinfulness and inadequacy and to discover the reality of God's forgiveness.

In the Easter services of the Holy Orthodox Church the liturgy builds up a picture of the sin of Adam and its consequence. Verse after verse tells of the awfulness of sin and the darkness of this world in its rebellion. Then the liturgy begins to speak of the coming of Christ, the second Adam. What the first Adam had lost through sin, the second Adam wins back. There begins a celebration of everything that the world has been given through Christ. The liturgy builds up to a climax until the sin of Adam is eclipsed by the overwhelming glory of what has been won by Christ and his cross. At last comes the astonishing line, 'O Happy Fault! – that won for us so great a salvation'!

There is a strange moral contradiction here, isn't there? Edwin Muir expressed this no less daringly when he wrote: 'It seems that in the love of God, in the love which is God, there is something which only sin can let us understand'.[1]

Sin among the coffee cups

'But I find it so hard to believe I can be forgiven, just like that', said someone to me recently. The Identikit workshop, mentioned in the last chapter, showed that many people find it easier to live with the knowledge that they are sinners than that they are forgiven. That has certainly been my experience and for many years my participation in church worship did little to challenge my attitude. Since childhood the pattern has been unchanging. Each Sunday the worship began with a hymn and then the Confession:

> Almighty God, our heavenly Father,
> we have sinned against you and against our
>   fellow men,
> in thought and word and deed,
> through negligence, through weakness,
> through our own deliberate fault.
> We are truly sorry and repent of all our sins.
> For the sake of your Son Jesus Christ, who
>   died for us,
> forgive us all that is past;
> and grant that we may serve you in newness
>   of life
> to the glory of your name.[2]

I would pray it and try to mean it. I listened to the words of absolution but nothing changed for me. And looking around me the services proceeded with no noticeable response of joy or release on hearing the news of God's mercy. We left the building the same people who had arrived an hour before. In one church a lay reader always finished the service with a prayer that closed with the words ' . . . and pardon all that thou hast seen of us'. Nothing *had* changed it seemed. Our sin was still firmly in the centre.

It is hard to believe that we have truly grasped the wonder of this forgiving. If that declaration of mercy in the service is true then it is startling news. It almost seems immoral to believe it. Indeed if it is not true then it is immoral and blasphemous (and for that very reason Jesus was crucified). But if it is true then it is not unlike a person sitting in a prison cell living under an indeterminate sentence with no hope of remission whose cell door is suddenly flung open and he or she is allowed to go home. In the Communion service a similar picture is used when we celebrate that God through Christ has 'freed us from the slavery of sin'. A more common difficulty in considering sin and forgiveness is that we all look such *nice* people! Sitting in Christian discussion groups, thoughtful, sincere and passing cups of coffee, doesn't all this talk of being 'miserable offenders' seem rather exaggerated? Of course, none of us is *perfect*, but are we really that bad? It is sometimes very hard to believe that if Jesus had lived in *our* town or community he would have needed to do anything so drastic as to die on a cross for us! It is not just our badness that we need saving from. It is our goodness. Sincere, religious people crucified the Lord of glory.

Making the break

While training at college I came to the conviction that confession and forgiveness were realities I had yet to grasp. I had never really felt like a sinner – and had never experienced a sense of forgiveness. Can you have one without the other? The emphasis on both in Christian evangelism has always made me rather uncomfortable or sceptical. But I had been reading Dietrich Bonhoeffer's book, *Life Together* and in one chapter he had this to say:

> In confession the breakthrough to community takes place. Since confession of sin is made in the presence of a Christian brother, the last stronghold of self-justification is abandoned. Confession in the presence of a brother is the profoundest kind of humiliation. It hurts, it cuts a man down, it is a dreadful blow to pride.
>
> In confession a man breaks through to certainty. Why is it that it is often easier for us to confess our sins to God than to a brother? God is holy and sinless, he is a judge of evil. But a brother is sinful as we are. He knows from his own experience the dark night of secret sin. Why should we not find it easier to go to a brother than to the holy God? But if

we do, we must ask ourselves with our confession of sin to God, whether we have not been confessing our sins to ourselves and also granting ourselves absolution. And is not the reason perhaps for our countless relapses and the feebleness of our Christian obedience to be found precisely in the fact that we are living on self-forgiveness and not a real forgiveness? Self-forgiveness can never lead to a breach with sin; this can be accomplished only by the judging and pardoning Word of God itself.[3]

His words made uncomfortable sense to me. I took a deep breath and I asked a close friend if I could come and pray with him, confessing my sins to God. I prepared quite a long list and we knelt together. For the first time in my life I felt ashamed of my sins and shortcomings. I felt overwhelmed with shame and my prayer was washed away on a flood of tears, conscious only of a longing for mercy and peace.

When I had calmed I heard from my friend the assurance of God's forgiveness. He took my list from me and tore it up. I heard him pray that in place of condemnation and sense of wrong, God would fill me with his Holy Spirit and inspire me to new life and attitudes. Then God spoke through him directly and I heard words of acceptance and delight in me that I scarcely believed. I left the room with a new assurance that I was a forgiven sinner.

Confession and absolution have never been the same since. It is not always emotional. More often it is quite matter-of-fact. But it always has the practical and objective sense of something being exchanged – things taken and things given.

True and false repentance

Without the liberating discovery that our worst is accepted by God and by each other, Christian life is a burdensome pretence. We learn to wear our masks that say we are strong and OK. We are unable to offer our real longings and needs. The tension in this pretence may express itself in different ways. A church that appears on the surface to be a friendly community may underneath be full of unhappy relationships and unresolved conflicts. Like Marcel Marceau's mime, it is a community trapped in its outward appearance. A church congregation only becomes a Christian community when it can admit its weaknesses and frailties together – when it discovers the forgiveness of sins. As Bonhoeffer wrote, 'It may be that Christians, notwithstanding corporate worship, common prayer, and all their fellowship in service, may still be left to their loneliness. The final breakthrough to fellowship does not occur, because, though they have fellowship with one another as believers and as devout people, they do not have fellowship as the undevout, as sinners'.[4]

But the breakthrough must go beyond the awareness of shared sinfulness, it must enter into the joy of God's acceptance and forgiveness. So much Christian living stops short of this. More disturbing than the deadly dullness of what is so often offered as Christian worship, is that people actually prefer it that way!

Unable to enter the liberty of true forgiveness we act out the pretence of having entered it (as in Marceau's mime), or we make a virtue of being unable to receive it, of our unworthiness. We cling to our solemnity believing that it is our means of acceptance by God. The former is the pretence of life that is actually death. The latter is the resisting of life by clinging to death. Gerard Hughes says that the real issue here is whether we have understood the difference between true and false repentance. He sums up the difference like this:

Marks of true repentance	*Marks of false repentance*
True repentance frees from self-preoccupation because our trust is in God's	False repentance immerses us in self-preoccupation. We delight in what we

goodness working in us. In his light we see our darkness.

consider our virtue but are irritated by our vice, refuse to acknowledge it and project it on to others.

True repentance brings joy and inner freedom.

False repentance increases anxiety and makes us more defensive.

True repentance can welcome criticism and learn from it.

False repentance is touchy about criticism and learns nothing from it.

True repentance brings understanding, tolerance and hope.

False repentance engenders a rigidity of mind and heart, dogmatism, intolerance and a condemnatory attitude.

True repentance brings compassion and therefore a sharpened sensitivity to all forms of injustice.

False repentance is sensitive to justice only in so far as it promotes the interest of the individual or his group and is therefore selective in its moral condemnation.

True repentance shares God's laughter and frees the mind to see the humour of situations.

False repentance tends to be over serious and cannot laugh at itself.

In true repentance a person feels drawn to God.

In false repentance a person feels driven by God.[5]

The fellowship of the forgiven

In deaf and dumb sign language, the word forgiveness is signed by wiping the palm of one hand firmly across the other as if removing any stain or mess that clings to it. This is exactly how the Bible speaks of forgiveness. Once God forgives, something has been wiped away, a relationship has been changed, old ways are discarded and new life begins. Forgiveness was such a holy and profound reality for the first Christians they were not sure what to do with people who obviously sinned again after receiving it. It was a particular pastoral problem after times of persecution. This was the origin of the sacrament of penance. Upon repentance, the fallen Christian would be prescribed acts of self-discipline, intended to strengthen him or her against falling into sin again.

An incident in the film *The Mission* illustrates our longing for and struggle with forgiveness and acceptance. Rodrigo Mendoza, a slave trader, has become a Christian through the care of Father Gabriel. He hears the assurance of God's forgiveness for his sins but he feels the need to act out his penitence. He wants to do penance for his sins. (The story also shows how easily penance can be a refusal of forgiveness by attempting to earn it.) He voluntarily journeys back into the Amazon jungle, to the peoples he had been kidnapping and murdering, dragging a heavy bundle of swords and guns. The route is long and hard. When he reaches the tribe, exhausted and filthy, he is immediately recognised and the chief approaches him with a knife. It is a moment of great tension. But the chief bends over Mendoza and cuts him free from his burden, pushing it over the cliff. Mendoza weeps and the tribe cluster around, holding him and wiping his tears. So the burden of his guilt is released and God's love becomes real through the acceptance of that Amazon tribe. He has entered the fellowship of the forgiven.

8

The Sign of Jonah

I was driving through torrential rain on the M40. It was a grey, miserable day and my mood matched it. A lorry overtook me. It was so covered with dirt and grime that I could hardly read the name of the firm that owned it. As it pulled in front of me I noticed that someone had written in the dirt across its back, 'Also available in white'!

That lorry and its improbable message illustrates God's attitude to this world. We are offered the promise, not just of a clean-up – but of transfiguration. God has written in the dust and grime of this world the words of eternal life. He persistently refuses to treat us as we deserve or leave us in our helplessness to change. He loves us in our dustiness and promises us glory.

Dust that dreams

We live with this contradiction deep within our nature. We are undeniably rooted in the sweat and decay of a passing world, yet we cannot surrender the outrageous hope of heaven. Someone put it like this:

I am dust and ashes, frail and wayward, riddled with fears,

beset with needs whose origins I do not understand and whose
satisfaction I cannot achieve . . . and unto dust I shall return.
Who can expect much of that? But there is something else in
me; there is an awareness that, truly, I am not what I am; and
that what I am not is what I truly am. Dust I may be,
but troubled dust, dust that dreams, dust that has strange
premonitions of transfiguration, of a glory in store, a destiny
prepared, an inheritance that will one day be my own. How
else do you account for all those fairy tales that characterise
our history? All those paupers who were really princes; all
those kitchen maids who were really a king's true love; all
those ugly ducklings who were majestic swans; all that glory
rising from cinders and ashes. So my life is stretched out in
a painful dialectic between ashes and glory, between weakness
and transfiguration. I am like the man in the old Jewish prov-
erb who had two texts in his pockets, one telling him he was
dust and ashes and the other that for him the whole of the
world was made.[1]

That much we can recognise in some measure. What is less
believable is the passionate longing which God has for this
dust. He has a love and desire that is not satisfied until he
has taken dust himself – become one with our human nature.
Rubem Alves once wrote, 'What the doctrine of the incar-
nation whispers to us is that God, eternally, wants a body
like ours'.[2] It all sounds so unlikely, doesn't it? We can cope
with the thought that God might want to clean us up or put
us on the right road again. But that God should find something desirable in this human nature, to the point of sharing
it at great cost – that is harder to take in.

It is at this point that so many of the traditional descriptions
of the cross of Christ fall short. As we noted in chapter 2,
Christian faith in Western Europe, with its roots in the order
and precision of the Roman Empire, has tended to prefer to
describe salvation in the language of legal and commercial
transactions. The Holy Orthodox Church has always chosen

a significantly different emphasis. They may be compared in this way:

WEST	EAST
On the cross Christ is paying the debt we owe for our sin. The death he dies is the price we owe.	Through the cross Christ restores relationships that have been broken: between God and his world; between peoples of the world.
On the cross Christ is the victim in our place, enduring our suffering.	On the cross Christ is the victor on our behalf, leading us to freedom.
Christ became a man and died on the cross to redeem us and put us right with God.	Christ became a man that we might become divine. He glorifies us and we share in the life of the Holy Trinity.
We have the cross because God must impose a punishment for sin. Christ took upon himself the sentence that God must impose upon the world.	We have the cross because God loves the world so much he provides the sacrifice himself. God was in Christ reconciling the world to himself.

Do you see the contrast in those columns (though both are 'true')? I have long wished that the Christian message I first responded to had had the personal warmth and inviting mystery of the Orthodox belief alongside the stern, divine Judge I met in Western theology. For many years, although I prayed 'our Father' I could never get out of the dock. Believing remained a very sterile and joyless experience.

Yet that right-hand column reminds us that God's deepest longing is for our union with him. The most moving passages in the Old Testament are those in which God speaks of himself as suffering like a rejected lover or deserted marriage partner. Like one who cannot help his love, he calls out to his world, willing to forgive without end and to suffer the cost of it.

In one example, Hosea is given a vision in which God sees the day coming when the relationship he longs for is going to be restored. Israel will return with new love and faithfulness to the covenant relationship they had with him. With the expansive enthusiasm of a lover, he sees all creation celebrating the event!

'I will lead her into the desert
 and speak tenderly to her . . .
There she will sing as in the days of her
 youth . . .
In that day,' declares the Lord,
 'you will call me "my husband";
 you will no longer call me "my master" . . .
In that day I will respond,'
 declares the Lord –
 'I will respond to the skies,
 and they will respond to the earth;
and the earth will respond to the grain,
 the new wine and oil,
 and they will respond to Jezreel . . .
I will show my love to the one I called "Not my loved
 one",
I will say to those called, "Not my people",
 "You are my people" and they will say, "You are my
 God".'

(Hosea 2:14, 15, 16, 21–2, 23)

The pursuing God

St Paul calls the life we receive from Christ an *arrabon*. The old Greek word means 'first instalment'. This relates to our experience of the gift of the Holy Spirit. It has the sense of a foretaste, of something yet to come. In modern Greek the same word means 'engagement ring'. God's mercy and love through Christ is a betrothal gift to the world. Far more than the paying off of debts or the settling of legal requirements, the cross is about the reawakening of love. On the cross Jesus is bringing together the two sides of a long lost relationship.

In these chapters on forgiveness we have been exploring the joy and pain of being accepted and loved. We have seen the way in which a world that hides from and fears love can only destroy real love when it is offered. This is the cross of Christ – 'love to the loveless shown that they might lovely be'.

But this love pursues us even through death. Nothing can stop it and nothing, in the end, can escape it.

> Where can I go from your Spirit?
>   Where can I flee from your presence?
> If I go up to the heavens, you are there;
>   if I make my bed in the depths,
>   you are there.
> If I rise on the wings of the dawn,
>   if I settle on the far side of the sea,
> even there your hand will guide me,
>   your right hand will hold me fast.
>   (Ps. 139:7–10)

Even in the beauty of these verses there is an ambivalence. The presence of this God is so all-embracing and all-consuming that we are never quite sure whether we want it or not. I have never understood the attraction of those plaques that some Christian families have on the wall of their dining-room:

> Christ is the head of this household,
> the silent listener to every conversation,
> the unseen guest at every meal.

It is a sentiment that makes me spend most of the meal wanting to check over my shoulder. I invariably leave the meal table with indigestion. I used to get the same sinking feeling at theological college when the football team insisted on starting each game with a prayer in the centre circle. I had no confidence that God liked football as much as I did – but I was very sure that he turned up to observe every foul and hear every swear word that escaped my lips during the game. He was always the referee, never one of the players. I knew that inviting God along should have increased my joy because, after all, I was a *Christian*. But I am glad now of the chance to confess that I never said 'Amen' and wished I had the courage to say, 'Leave God out of it and let's enjoy the game!' I think David the psalmist would have understood.

The same uncertainty about being constantly observed can be one of the most uncomfortable adjustments in the early days of marriage. Loving is a terribly uncertain enterprise in a world like ours. We have learned to erect defences to protect ourselves. And when the eternal God says he loves us, what are we to think? What can dust and glory have in common? This is a meeting of complete opposites – time and eternity, dust and glory, sin and holiness, God and humanity. Can it work? Are we compatible or will we just get hurt? But if it is all true and 'possible' then we are being drawn into a relationship beyond our imagining.

The sign of contradiction

'If you want to find your handsome prince you have to kiss a lot of toads', the saying goes. So what does it feel like to be kissed by God? Certainly not what we imagine it to be. For the cross of Jesus is a perpetual reminder that God's love must constantly surprise us, shock us or comfort us. It doesn't matter which, as long as love breaks through our defences somehow. Our images of God will be constantly contradicted and renewed. Within this strange relationship we will struggle with all our uncertain experience of loving and living, all our wounded perceptions about our self-worth, all our seeking and fleeing from God. And the cross tells us how deeply and lovingly God wrestles with us too.

A prayer group once meditated on the armour of God (Ephesians chapter 6). The leader encouraged the group to imagine putting on each piece of armour as he mentioned them – the helmet of salvation, the sword of the Spirit. When it came to the belt of truth a woman in the group began to weep quietly and afterwards told of her experience. 'When you told us to put the belt on, you emphasised how important it was for holding all the uniform together. It was the belt of *truth*. All I could see in my mind was a tatty scored length of leather on the point of falling apart. I knew that was me, worn out and worthless. I began to weep. Then you said, look at the buckle on your belt. I saw the most beautiful buckle. An exquisite piece of metal work. I couldn't understand how it ever came to be part of my belt. I knew the buckle was Christ. You told us to put the belt on. I hardly dared put my tatty belt into that buckle but when I did it fitted perfectly.'

'Forgiveness is at the heart of the universe', wrote Bishop Stephen Neill. The point of acceptance of our deepest divisions and needs becomes the place where love and life are restored. Christ on the cross, hanging between earth and heaven, between dust and glory, between curse and blessing, enables a universal meeting and reconciling.

And forgetting

Christian love is not only a forgiving but a forgetting as well. In our experiences of being wronged we often insist, 'I can forgive but I cannot forget'. But God insists that no forgiveness is final until all remembering of the sin or hurt is healed. This capacity to forget makes the restored relationship complete. So when God describes, through Jeremiah, a new relationship with his world in which 'all will know me, from the least of them to the greatest', he links it to forgiveness *and forgetting* – 'For I will forgive their wickedness and will remember their sins no more' (31:34). So in our encounter with God's love there is to be a beginning that eclipses all that is past. For a glory is revealed in us that covers all that has gone before (Rom. 8:18ff). In the splendour of this love there is no looking back. Can anything so loved in heaven have ever been the dust of earth? Can anything so full of grace have ever been cursed by sin?

Thomas Merton wrote of this paradox at the close of his journal, *The Sign of Jonas*. The prophet Jonah was always a sign to him of the mystery and contradiction of the journey into God's love and will. Jonah was a man who found himself going where God wanted him despite fleeing in the opposite direction! The mystery of his calling by God was lived out in the darkness of the belly of the whale.

The Voice of God is heard in Paradise:

'What was vile has become precious. What is now precious was never vile. I have always known the vile as precious: for what is vile I know not at all. What was cruel has become merciful. What is now merciful was never cruel. I have always overshadowed Jonas with my mercy, and cruelty I know not at all. Have you had sight of Me, Jonas my Child? Mercy within mercy within mercy. I have forgiven the universe without end, because I have never known sin.

What was poor has become infinite. What was infinite was never poor. I have always known poverty as infinite: riches I love not at all. Prisons within prisons within prisons. Do not lay up for yourselves ecstasies upon earth, where time and space corrupt, where the minutes break in and steal. No more lay hold upon time, Jonas, My son, lest the rivers bear you away. What was fragile has become powerful. I loved what was most frail. I looked upon what was nothing. I touched what was without substance, and within what was not, I am.'[3]

PART C

Whose Death Do You
See There?

'take up your cross and follow me'

9

The Forsaken Night

From the sixth hour until the ninth hour darkness came over all the land. About the ninth hour Jesus cried out in a loud voice, 'Eloi, Eloi, lama sabachthani' – which means, 'My God, my God, why have you forsaken me?'

(Matt. 27:45–6)

Where is God now?

One day when we came back from work, we saw three gallows rearing up in the assembly place, three black crows. Roll call. SS all round us, machine guns trained: the traditional ceremony. Three victims in chains – and one of them, the little servant, the sad eyed angel.

The SS seemed more preoccupied, more disturbed than usual. To hang a young boy in front of hundreds of spectators was no light matter. The head of the camp read the verdict. All eyes were on the child. He was lividly pale, almost calm, biting his lips. The gallows threw its shadow over him . . .

The three victims mounted together on to the chairs.

The three necks were placed at the same moment within the nooses . . .

'Where is God? Where is He?' someone behind me asked.

At a sign from the head of the camp, the three chairs tipped over.

Total silence throughout the camp. On the horizon the sun was setting.

'Bare your heads!' yelled the head of the camp. His voice was raucous. We were weeping.

'Cover your heads!'

Then the march past began. The two adults were no longer alive. Their tongues hung swollen, blue-tinged. But the third rope was still moving; being so light, the child was still alive . . .

For more than half an hour he stayed there, struggling between life and death, dying in slow agony under our eyes. And we had to look him full in the face. He was still alive when I passed in front of him. His tongue was still red, his eyes were not yet glazed.

Behind me I heard the same man asking:

'Where is God now?'

And I heard a voice within me answer him:

'Where is He? Here He is – He is hanging here on this gallows . . . '[1]

Did that thought bring comfort to Elie Wiesel as he watched that child? He doesn't tell us. And if God *is* there, who would dare draw near him? In the midst of the Holocaust we are introduced to a God whose presence in this world is still found on a gallows.

I find it hard to speak of the cross as God's 'answer' to the world. Firstly because such language tends to oversimplify both the glory and the pain of what is going on there. And secondly, because we human beings tend to stop looking when we are given answers. We make our bed on answers and there we rest content. Answers close doors. Questions open them. When Karl Marx called Religion the opium of the people he didn't mean that it was a drug that filled us

with an illusory sense of meaning. He meant that we tend
to use religion to anaesthetise us from having to face the
deepest questions. It can enable us comfortably to close off
from having to feel pain.

How many of the official liturgies of the Church of England lead worshippers into pain-bearing prayer for starving
peoples or to share the cries of the torture victims? We have
yet to recover the power of protest and lament that fill the
Hebrew psalms. We are a people who have lost the ability
to weep – if not for ourselves then for those around us. The
following poem came in a moment of fury at the end of a
Sunday morning when I had read horrific details of suffering
in the newspaper and then sat through what seemed the
bland, remote comfort of a Christian service of Holy Communion. When I was offered the wine from the silver chalice
I suddenly remembered the words of Jesus on the cross – 'I
thirst'.

> I thirst
> and should I not
> in such a world as this?
>
> I thirst for justice from the prison cells,
> for springs to fill the village wells,
>
> I thirst the love that heals the broken things,
> for famine's end on monsoon winds,
>
> I am the tear that mourns the broken trust,
> I am the seed that's withered in the dust,
>
> For all that lives and dies in fear
> I thirst a day when hope draws near.
>
> Don't stem the rivers of my dreams

or mock me with your heavenly drink
don't run to touch my lips with wine

for I must thirst
in such a world
as this.

The question why

Without ever answering the question 'why' the cross of
Christ reveals a God who is passionately and painfully
involved in this world. He shares the dirt, the sweat, the
loneliness, the weakness and even death itself. We face
nothing worse than he was prepared to endure himself. Not
that that knowledge completely satisfies us. We may still
wish this gospel offered something less costly. Who hasn't
felt torn between a longing that God would simply be all-
powerful and 'make it better' and the realisation that God
could only do that by undoing all that he has created us to
be – with the terrible freedoms and choices that make us
human beings. In the first instance God is not 'the answer to
it all' – for he has clearly chosen not to wave the wand over
this world and make it all right. But he is 'God with us' in
it all.

So completely has God entered into this human life that
Jesus can teach that every act of compassion and love offered
to the needy is actually offered to him (Matt. 25:40). Where
is he? He is here, in the face of the starving child, the cells
of the torture victims, the desolation of the homeless family,
the bitter rejection of the AIDS victim. Contradictory though
it sounds, God is even present at times when he is absent
and life feels utterly deserted. For on the cross Jesus has even
entered the absence of God with us – 'why have you forsaken
me?'

Jesus also taught that we will be judged by whether we

loved him through the poor, the homeless and the needy.
The Jesus of the cross made his home among the abandoned
and forsaken. To reject them is to reject him (Matt.
25:31–46). However hard we find the question of suffering,
the God of the cross asks that, like him, we live in the heart
of it.

Sheila Cassidy, from her personal experience of torture in
a Chilean jail and in her work among the terminally ill, has
lived long with the problem of suffering. In her moving book
Good Friday People she describes the place she has reached.

> I have long since given up asking the 'why' of suffering. It
> gets me nowhere, and I know when I'm beat. I live quite
> peaceably in the eye of the theological storm, moving about
> in the accustomed darkness like a mole in its burrow or a
> blind woman in the safety of her home . . . But this I *do*
> know: more important than asking why we should get in
> there, be alongside those who suffer. We must plunge in up
> to our necks in the icy water, the mud and the slurry to hold
> up the drowning child until he is rescued or dies in our arms.
> If he dies, so be it, and if we die with him, so be it also.
> Greater love hath no man, than he who lays down his life for
> his friend.[2]

Dietrich Bonhoeffer believed the same. Imprisoned and
finally executed in the Second World War he struggled to
understand God's ways in the midst of political corruption
and violence. He too believed the question 'why' was unpro-
ductive. Instead of asking 'why is God allowing this to
happen?' we should be asking 'where is God at work in what
is happening?' The first question leads us nowhere practical.
Through the second question we enter what is happening
and may find ways to respond to it.

But in the raw pain of human suffering even this discussion
seems remote. The protests will still erupt from our depths
as they did for the psalmist. We struggle with the absence of
God and the prospering of evil.

Why do you stand far off, O Lord!
why do you hide your face in time of need!
The ungodly in their pride persecute the poor
. . . and secretly murder the innocent
the upright are crushed and humbled before
him
Arise O Lord God! Lift up your hand.
                              (Ps. 10 from 1–13)

There is so much darkness and pain in this world that must
simply be 'lived with' – borne without hope or sign of
change. At such times, if we are able, we wait with the
chaos, in the eye of the storm, under the dark sky beside
the cross and the crucified love which no darkness could
overcome. We hold to the conviction that all this was made
for something better. In the night we cling, with all the
strength in our being, to the conviction that we are:

a unique and beautiful creation
of which these things are no part.[3]

Sharing the darkness

For those of us who can choose, such a sharing in suffering
will feel daunting and beyond us. Sheila Cassidy comments
on how 'people on the outside of the caring world look
nervously in and say, "Aren't you wonderful! I do admire
you. I could never do anything like that"'. But she makes
the simple point that caring begins with very ordinary people
responding with very small acts of love. Slowly they are
drawn in more deeply. Compassion is God's strength and
love given to people who know their weakness.

One of the hardest things about sharing the sufferings of
others is the feeling of helplessness. We long to be able to *do*
something. We may have to face the question of whether

our longing for a solution is more to satisfy the terror of our powerlessness. But if we accept our helplessness for what it is we become, in that moment, a fellow sufferer. Real caring begins in letting go of our need to be the 'strong' helping the 'weak' – for it is no such thing. For in the meeting of mutual pain and longing suffering itself may be a teacher.

When Carl Jung worked on the staff of a mental hospital in Zurich there was a woman who was regarded as incurable. She never spoke. There was something threatening about her silence. She spent her days alone, often in the hospital gardens. Jung's colleagues warned him against her. There was no hope for her; she was possibly dangerous. But he refused to believe this. He watched her from a distance, and tried to imagine her feelings, to enter her world. One day he came across her sitting in the garden. She was making certain odd movements. Jung had an irresistible urge to go and sit beside her, make the same movements as her for a while, then close his eyes and say whatever came into his head. He did just that and, not without anxiety, spoke a few words. After a short pause he heard a low feminine voice ask, 'But how did you know?'

From that moment a relationship was formed. Within six months the woman was discharged from the hospital.[4]

This is the way of the cross. And we are to learn to love the way God loves. We are to draw near to each other, to move to each other's pain, to stumble in each other's darkness. And in the void, in the eye of the storm, we dare to trust that Christ hangs there too, in our midst, becoming all that we are enduring.

10

The Wounds of Loving

'The longer I go on the more I wonder why anyone chooses to be a Christian. Who wants to be a martyr?' said a friend recently. 'Gospel' means Good News, but on the lips of Jesus this 'Good News' is uncompromising stuff – 'If any man would come after me, let him deny himself and take up his cross and follow me' (Mark 8:34 RSV). The only people who carry their own crosses are those who have been condemned to death. They are walking the few yards from Death Row to the place of execution. What use are personal ambitions and career plans at such a time? The picture is a stark one. As Dietrich Bonhoeffer once wrote, 'When Christ calls a man he bids him come and die'. No one can accuse Jesus of attracting followers the easy way. I have seen some tough, challenging recruitment posters for the British Armed Forces but none has ever carried the caption, 'Join the army and die!'

Strange blessing

The lifestyle Jesus outlines for his followers is no less demanding. For although he insists that these are people who are blessed by God, they are hungry, thirsty, poor, meek, in mourning, merciful, persecuted and somehow able to bring peace (Matt. 5:3–12)! But having come so far in our reflections on the cross of Christ we should not be so surprised. The late Dr Frank Lake, out of his work with people desperately wounded in their search for life and God, would even describe the cross as 'God's apology' for the suffering life has inflicted on them.

St Paul says that Christians are like brittle clay pots whose lives somehow contain a priceless treasure. His experience of taking up the cross sounds very close to the mixture of blessing and adversity that Jesus asks of his followers.

> We have this treasure in jars of clay to show that this all-surpassing power is from God and not from us. We are hard pressed on every side, but not crushed; perplexed, but not in despair; persecuted, but not abandoned; struck down, but not destroyed. We always carry around in our body the death of Jesus, so that the life of Jesus may be revealed in our body. For we who are alive are always being given over to death for Jesus' sake, so that his life may be revealed in our mortal body. So then, *death is at work in us, but life is at work in you.* (my italic 2 Cor. 4:7–12)

As someone once observed, if the blessing of God in the Old Testament is seen in prosperity, the blessing of God in the New Testament is seen through adversity.

There is nothing less attractive than a Christian community that is trying to be holy and loving by its own efforts. The effect has all the attractiveness and appeal of disinfectant. It kills everything. But the cross-centred community, Good Friday people, know their frailty and capacity for lovelessness. They know their hunger and poverty, and mourn for the wounds of this world and their part in them. Christian saints are not the most faultless people – they are the most forgiven.

I lived in a large community for five years, the Lee Abbey community in North Devon. Although many of the guests assumed that life together as Christians must be heaven it was often hell! You soon lose the illusion of your own tolerance and Christian virtue sharing your life with sixty other people. But I noticed how often, when life in community seemed hardest and most painful, I would meet guests who had clearly received God's love in a special way. At first I was tempted to be cynical. But this is what St Paul was describing. He understood that any struggles for the sake of the gospel somehow released life to others. 'Death is at work in us, but life is at work in you.'

It is hard not to want to be the treasure rather than the lumpy, flawed clay pot that contains it. I once listened to the story of a guest on a special holiday for single-parent families. Her story was one of appalling adversity. Nothing in life had gone right for her. Every hope had been dashed and every dream betrayed. As I listened I sank into depression. I couldn't understand how she was still a Christian. But I also felt terribly helpless. I was a priest. I should have something to say. But what she was describing was hell and I was sinking there with her.

She turned to me with her weary face and asked, 'Where is God in all that?' Feeling as if I was betraying Lee Abbey, the Church of England, Christ and God, I said, 'I don't know.'

She touched my arm and laughed. 'It's so nice to talk to someone who hasn't got all the answers!'

I laughed too and somehow weights dropped off us both in that moment.

Burden of victory

While studying at college I once attended a lecture on the theme of salvation and the victory of the cross. I remember only one moment from the talk. The lecturer looked up from his notes, as if moved by a sudden thought and said, 'You know, sometimes a colleague comes into the office first thing in the morning and says "Praise the Lord!" – and I just want to kick him in the balls!' I knew exactly what he meant.

The Christian Church proclaims that on the cross Christ is both the pain bearer for the world and also the victor over sin and suffering. There is a tension here that is not easy to live with. Victory and pain seem almost a contradiction. Christians have tended to live with one truth or the other. It is hard to live with both. The following drama opens up this tension for group discussion. The two scripts are read loudly and simultaneously. A is sitting on the back of B who is kneeling on the floor on hands and knees.

A: Lord, we praise you for your victory on the cross. By your suffering and death you have won the victory! We praise you that sin and death are no more and that our lives can be full of your love. We praise you that your presence heals all our diseases. You make us whole. It is your will that we should live in your victory. Thank you that nothing separates us from your love and that day by day your mercies are renewed to us. We praise you and celebrate your love among us!

B: I am hurting. I am still hurting! God, why aren't I healed? I am tired of praying and trying to believe. It is so hard to trust. Nothing works for me. Where are you God? Why have you forsaken me? I just want someone to be with me in this. I just want someone to talk to. It's so lonely. They all look so whole and full of faith. It hurts God! What am I supposed to do? And all they do is sing choruses.

We must be careful how we use the word 'victory'. It is not always obvious that a victory is good news in a world like ours. It may replace one injustice with another. When in 1991, the Western forces won the victory to liberate Kuwait it was soon clear that the immediate result was even greater suffering. It is equally true that a people liberated from an experience of oppression and suffering may not have learned compassion or justice through their experience. After the same war Amnesty International reported that the returning Kuwaiti government was taking revenge with torture and killings as brutal as that of the Iraqis.

From a country that has known appalling suffering come the sober words of an Israeli journalist. Uri Avneri's comments were made in the context of his government's policies in the Lebanon.

> I will tell you . . . it would be nice to believe that people who have undergone suffering have been purified by suffering. But it's the opposite, it makes them worse. It corrupts. There is something in suffering that creates a kind of egoism. You get a kind of moral power-of-attorney . . . because nothing can compare with what has happened to us.[1]

With its own long history of divisions, bigotry and bloodshed, the Christian church itself is eloquent witness to its own need for conversion. How many aircraft carriers and nuclear submarines have been blessed with the sign of the cross and the victory of Christ? We should not be surprised. It was devoutly religious people who crucified Jesus. Bad religion is surely worse than no religion at all. Now, as then, 'Jesus on the cross represents an identity we crucify rather than enter'.[2]

Into the paschal candle on Easter night the church fixes five grains of incense – representing the wounds of Christ – with the words 'by his holy and glorious wounds, may Christ our Lord guard us and keep us'. The victory at the cross is primarily the victory of compassion over hatred, of freedom to weep for one's enemies, of finding the courage and grace to embrace suffering. Firstly, because that is what love demands. Secondly, because only there, only in Christ, was such pain endured and overcome without reprisal or despair.

Living as one

> Pray not for Arab or Jew,
> for Palestinian or Israeli,
> but pray rather for yourselves
> that you may not divide them in your prayers
> but keep them both together in your hearts.[3]

This prayer touches something very important in Christian praying and living. So often if I remember to pray for someone I don't like I still pray for them apart from me. My prayer confirms my divisions. How can we be physically reconciled to someone that our hearts are still divided from? In Ephesians we are told that Christ on the cross has brought all that was divided together. 'For he himself is our peace, who has made the two one and has destroyed the barrier, the dividing wall of hostility' (Eph. 2:14). Christians are to live and pray as if that is true.

In a world like ours this will often mean holding on in the dark; holding to the hope that a situation must change. To illustrate this I think of a remarkable story from Chile's recent past. Under General Pinochet's long dictatorship many people suffered torture, execution or just simply disappeared. Mothers, wives and daughters of missing loved ones would gather daily in the city square. Their protest took a particular form. They danced the Gueca Solo – danced alone as if their loved one were there in their arms.[4] In so doing they brought together, in love and protest, that which was separated. They acted out their hope and faith of a different tomorrow.

I close this chapter with another picture of cross-bearing love. It comes from the 'ordinariness' of family conflict (though the late R. D. Laing insisted, in his provocative way, that 'normal' life is always the most dangerous!). The context of the story is perhaps more surprising.

Chaim Potok wrote a novel about a Jewish boy brought up in a strict orthodox home in Brooklyn. From his earliest days he had to draw. He drew brilliantly. He was a prodigy. His father could not understand his gift and opposed it as evil. His mother, a frail, sensitive woman was torn between her husband and son. They only really met through her. Against his father's wishes he was allowed to train as an artist. But the pain of his home life never left him and he finally had to find a way of expressing it. He began a painting:

I drew the frame of the living-room window in our Brooklyn apartment. I drew the strip of wood that divided the window and the slanting bottom of the Venetian blind a few inches from the top of the window. On top I drew my mother in her housecoat, with her arms extended along the horizontal of the blind, her wrists tied to it with the cords of the blind, her legs tied at the ankles to the vertical of the inner frame with another section of the cord blind. I arched her body and twisted her head. I drew my father standing to her right, dressed in a hat and coat and carrying an attaché case. I drew myself standing to her left, dressed in paint-spattered clothes and a fisherman's cap and holding a palette and holding a spear-like brush. I exaggerated the size of the palette and balanced it by exaggerating the size of my father's attaché case. We were looking at my mother and at each other. I split my mother's head into balanced segments, one looking at me, one looking at my father, one looking upward. The torment, the tearing anguish I felt in her, I put into her mouth, into the twisting curve of her head, the arching of her slight body, the clenching of her small fists, the taut downward pointing of her thin legs. I sprayed fixative on the charcoal and began to put on the colours . . . I painted swiftly in a strange nerveless frenzy of energy. For all the pain you suffered, my mama. For all the torment of your past and future years, my mama. For all the anguish this picture of pain will cause you. For the unspeakable mystery that brings good fathers and sons into the world and lets a mother watch them tear at each other's throats. For the Master of the Universe, whose suffering world I do not comprehend. For dreams of horror, for nights of waiting, for memories of death, for the love I have for you, for all the things I remember, and for all the things I should remember but have forgotten, for all these I created this painting – an observant Jew working on a crucifixion.[5]

11

Against the Grain

A young priest is sent to a remote Indian fishing village in British Columbia. It is a depressed community. The young are restless. Old ways are being forgotten. The traditions are dying.

His story is told in the novel *I Heard the Owl Call My Name*.[1] Late in September he climbs with Keetah, a village girl, to the source of the river above the village. The salmon are spawning and he wants to see the end of the 'swimmers' as the Indians call them. This is a significant journey in the book, for Father Mark is yet to discover that he carries terminal cancer within him and his young companion embodies the tension of old and new ways in her village. Together they watch the female swimmer digging the seed beds with her torn tail, her fins battered and worn. She lays her eggs and waits for the male to cover them with milt. Salmon are among those species in creation whose acts of life-giving, love-making are also their moment of dying.

They moved again and saw the end of the swimmer. They watched her last valiant fight for life, her struggle to right herself when the gentle stream turned her, and they watched the water force open her gills and draw her slowly downstream, tail first, as she had started life as a fingerling. In Keetah's eyes there were tears.

'It is always the same,' she said, 'the end of the swimmer is sad.'

'But Keetah, it isn't,' said Mark. 'The whole adventure of the swimmer is one of courage and adventure. All of it builds to the climax and the end. When the swimmer dies he has spent himself completely for the end for which he was made, and this is not sadness. It is triumph.'

The shadow of death

I often remember those words when I take funeral services. For I am never more aware than at such times of how profoundly our society has lost touch with the reality of death. We have become experts at prolonging life but we are unable to face its ending. When it comes we are unprepared. We meet it as a stranger, shaken and bruised by its brutal invasion of our world.

As far as we are able, we remove death from daily life. We disguise it in our conversation too – the dead have 'slipped away', 'passed on' or 'fallen asleep'. But death is too great a certainty to be evaded so easily. Until we turn and accept the reality of death, the struggle to evade it can only drain us and rob us of life. No one who clings to life 'for dear life' (which is actually for fear of death) is really free to live at all. The fear of death is already death.

Jesus struggled with death. At the tomb of Lazarus he is seen to weep and wrestle with deep emotion (John 11:33 and 38). It also seems quite possible that Joseph died before Jesus began his adult ministry, so he lived through family bereavement. We know that Jesus lived his own life with a constant awareness of his own approaching death. He knew it would be violent and horrific. How painful this knowledge was to him we only glimpse in the climax of his struggle in the

Garden of Gethsemane. He knew his own mortality and that his life must find its meaning in the will and gift of God. But woven into his earthly life was the unique calling to live and die for the world. He would choose to lay down his life. His dying would be the climax of his living. It would not be a 'tragedy' or 'untimely'. In St John's Gospel Jesus even calls it his 'glorifying' (chapter 17).

From early in his ministry he tried to prepare the disciples for his approaching death. On one occasion, immediately after Peter's declaration that Jesus was 'the Christ', Jesus 'began to teach them that the Son of Man must suffer many things and be rejected by the elders, chief priests and teachers of the law, and that he must be killed and after three days rise again.' We then read that Peter took him aside and began to rebuke him. This was not what should happen to Messiahs! Jesus reacted violently. He turned and rebuked Peter as the Devil himself. 'You do not have in mind the things of God but the things of men' (Mark 8:33).

Why was he so angry? Peter had meant well, hadn't he? How was he to know better? And it is not immediately clear what the rebuke actually means. Although Peter is called the Devil he is not told his thoughts come from hell but from earth. Certainly Peter, in his ignorance, was trying to turn Jesus away from the very thing he came to do – to give his life for the world. He is rebuked for resisting the will of God. But there is more to it. What Peter was resisting was not just the way that Jesus had to go. He was resisting *his own road*. So Jesus goes on to tell the disciples that they too must choose the way of the cross. There is no other way. 'For whoever wants to save his life will lose it, but whoever loses his life for me and for the gospel will save it. What good is it for a man to gain the whole world, yet forfeit his soul?' (Mark 8:34)

Losing and finding

It may be that the worst evils in our world are born out of this flight. Our drives to possess, to own, to control, to become self-sufficient, all look very foolish in the light of our mortality. If we allow it to, death will put life into a quite new perspective.

Morris West's novel, *Lazarus*,[2] is built around the experience of a crusty, ageing legalistic Pope who has to undergo major heart surgery. He is suddenly faced with death and the fact of his mortality. The experience changes him profoundly, as it does many people. In his struggle to allow the doctors to treat him he faces the fact he has never entrusted his life to anyone – not even to God. He has no option – and no strength to resist anyway. He is no longer in control. Even the Pope has no choice but to let a nurse hold the bottle to his penis so that he can urinate. In his physical vulnerability he discovers strange emotions within him that frighten and disturb him. But his visitors begin to find in him moments of unexpected feeling and even compassion. He comes to see that he has, through his encounter with death, passed into life for the first time. He has been born again and his approach to his life and work takes a radically new direction.

But there is no comfortable way of discovering this truth. The terror of death is in the not knowing. And in the moment of letting go there may be no glimmer of anything new or living to replace it.

It is not only in the dramatic moments of life that we are faced with death. We meet it in the daily round of ordinary life. In our response to the basic demands of living, possessing and relating, the reality of death constantly challenges our priorities, though we may try and ignore it.

Letting go

When I moved to London after some years living away from cities, I remember being overwhelmed by the speed of the traffic. Two years on I am driving as fast as anyone, but I soon began to realise that the traffic was a metaphor for life itself. People's diaries were as crowded and frantic as the roads. Now it is one thing to want to live life to the full. God wants that too. But this lifestyle felt *driven*. It was stressful. People told me as much, sometimes in tears.

We planned a series of sermons and discussion groups at church entitled 'Faith in the fast lane'. We all bewailed our busy-ness. We spoke longingly of creating silence and space in the diary. But the most important question was the hardest to face: 'just why *are* we running so hard?' In my experience from leading retreats and quiet days the answer seems to be, 'If I stop I am terrified there will be nothing there'. We are back, in effect, to the fear of death.

Another feature of our society is its possessiveness. We are a culture marked by strong addictions – drugs, drink, food, people or *things*. Where I live jumble sales raise large amounts of money. But the quantity of jumble never goes down. I strongly suspect we have invented a respectable way of swopping possessions with each other under the guise of giving to charity! We avoid leaving any space in our lives for too long.

I had to face this for myself when I recently tried to reduce my library. I hadn't touched many of the volumes for years. But I found it almost impossible to throw any away! It was too painful. I liked the way they filled my shelves. It wasn't anything to do with reading them. Over a long beer I tried to ask myself some honest questions. The truth was I had never felt very confident of my intellectual ability. The pain of academic failure at school was still with me. My extravagant library was an image. An attempt to compensate for intellectual and personal insecurity. Dismantling even a little of it felt like death. It still does.

We meet the same anxiety in our human relationships. Within the joyful experience of falling in love there can also be an awakening of deep fearfulness. Our inner world is being invaded. We are losing our privacy. This is not in our control. For something as great and central as human love to enter our lives a space must be created somewhere. So someone described the feeling of 'whole areas inside being demolished'! The experience of love is also an experience of dying for it requires our complete self-giving. Equally the building and strengthening of a relationship requires a willingness to admit to the loveless, fearful and untrusting parts within. No love will survive by clinging only to the good bits.

The painful truth at the heart of the gospel is what also makes it Good News. Where death is confessed and embraced and entered, there new life will emerge.

The gift of death

It was for this reason that St Francis always spoke of his friend 'Sister Death'. She was, for him, a constant companion on the road of life. In her company life found its true perspective, joyfully and deeply. In her company it was less tempting to cling to lesser things. It was pointless to possess. She reminds us that life is a gift, that it is for giving not for owning. In the company of Sister Death all life jumps sharply into focus. Have you considered this? Without death nothing has any more importance than anything else. It will all happen in the end. Nothing really matters. Life becomes an endless sequence of events without priority. Therefore thank God for death.

It is no coincidence that St Francis is remembered for his compassion. When we are no longer preoccupied with our own survival then there is a new space in our lives for belonging and caring for each other. There is nothing triumphalist about it. It is a gift of grace that we always experience as a severe mercy.

Donald Nicholl tells of someone lying in fear and desolation in a hospital bed. He was critically ill and afraid, and knew only that his world had all but died.

> Nothing of his true self seemed to remain except a tiny particle the size of a grain of mustard seed. Outside that particle all was chaos and darkness. Suddenly he heard a voice from the nearby corridor: 'I'm that bloody lonely I could cry.' It was the voice of an old miner who was in hospital for the first time in his life . . . Hearing the terror in the old man's voice the desperately ill man . . . from the pit of his own terror . . . said to himself: 'I'll go out and sit by him if it's the last thing I do.' And he did. And from that moment his own terror began to lift . . . in the voice of the old man he had heard the call of God calling him to wholeness and holiness. You can begin anytime, anywhere, even if you are only a grain of mustard seed lying in a pit of terror.[3]

Jesus chose the same image to speak of the necessity of death to gain life: 'Unless a grain of wheat falls to the ground and dies, it remains only a single seed. But if it dies, it produces many seeds. The man who loves his life will lose it, while the man who hates his life in this world will keep it for eternal life' (John 12:24–5). These are uncomfortable words though – and they were uncomfortable for Jesus too. In the next breath he confesses his struggle to offer himself in just that way. 'Now my heart is troubled, and what shall I say? "Father save me from this hour?" No, it was for this very reason I came to this hour. Father, glorify your name!'

Some months ago I was asked to visit a man in an old people's home. He was very ill and had asked to see a priest. The staff said that he had never shown any religious interest before. I went as soon as I could but by the time I reached his bedside a stroke had taken away his speech. I sat helplessly as he tried to speak. He seemed full of some memory or incident and longed to be rid of it. I held his hand and watched his tears of frustration and the weight of some unspoken burden heavy on his face. Not knowing what he might understand by my words I prayed for him: for the lifting of his burden onto the cross of Christ and for his peace.

On my way home, full of pain, three thoughts wove their way into my grief. I cannot say they comforted me, but there was a sober strength and truth in them that promised life. I remembered the words of Jim Eliot, who was to lose his life as a Christian missionary in the Amazon: 'Make sure that when the time comes to die, all you have to do is die'. I found myself praying from the ancient Christian litany, 'From violence, murder, and dying unprepared – Good Lord, deliver us'. And I heard the words of Jesus: 'Take up your cross . . . '

12

The Bones

The lights were dimmed. Candles glowed around the room. A low voice began to chant:

> The hand of the Lord was upon me,
> he brought me out by the Spirit of the Lord
> and set me in the middle of a valley;
> it was full of dry bones . . .

He was chanting chapter 37 of the book of Ezekiel, the vision of the valley of dry bones. This was Good Friday evening. Christ had been laid in the tomb. We were celebrating the liturgy of the Orthodox Church. Every Orthodox Christian knows 'The Bones'!

> 'Son of man, can these bones live?'
> I said, 'O Sovereign Lord, you alone know.' (v. 3)

With every few verses the cantor raised his voice a semi-tone, building, with the original vision, to its dramatic climax.

> 'Come from the four winds, O breath,
> breathe into these slain, that they may live.'
> . . . and breath entered them;

they came to life and stood on their feet
– a vast army. (vv. 9, 10)

At the close of the liturgy the priest spoke to us.

'Look into the tomb', said the priest. 'God cannot die! Who do you see lying there? Look into the tomb. God cannot die. Whose death is he dying?'

The answer came to me with an almost frightening intensity. And not just for me. Sitting beside me was a man who was critically ill with a brain tumour. I had watched his thoughtful, suffering face all week. Now his eyes were moist with recognition.

Keeping secrets

'Don't you know that all of us who were baptised into Christ Jesus were baptised into his death?' wrote St Paul (Rom. 6:3). In the early days of the Church, baptism always took place on Easter Day. Christian converts were carefully prepared for some weeks beforehand (which is the origin of the season of Lent). The baptistry was a room off the church. Candidates entered the water naked, and they were immersed three times in the name of the Holy Trinity. Their old identity died in that water. Like new-born babies they passed through the waters, were named, clothed and fed (Holy Communion).

The conviction that being a Christian means dying into Christ's death and rising is at the heart of the New Testament. Paul writes of it as a literal event. Reminding his readers that they have received new life he says, 'Set your minds on things above, not on earthly things. For you died, and your life is now hidden with Christ in God. When Christ, who is your life, appears, then you also will appear with him in glory' (Col. 3:2–4). The same picture of being hidden and protected in God occurs in John's letters. He points out that

although we are now children of God, 'what we will be has
not yet been made known. But we know that when he
appears, we shall be like him' (1 John 3:2–3). So becoming
a Christian means entrusting to God the secret of who we
are becoming!

I was invited to visit a man some weeks before Christmas.
He had no church connections and I only found out later that
he had a life-long antipathy towards religious belief. On
meeting him he told me he had perhaps three more weeks
to live. He had known for at least a year that his cancer was
terminal. He spoke of his death with rare openness but he
was also full of questions. He asked me what I thought about
all the sufferings in the world. I took a deep breath and told
him that I had no answers but that I believed, in the words
of the Communion service, that Christ had 'opened wide his
arms for us on the cross' and that his love embraced all
suffering and dying. I told him that I believed that the cross
revealed how God always reaches out to us in this life, though
often we are unaware of it. I felt very inadequate and tongue-
tied but the thought moved him deeply. 'If that's true', I
said, 'then God is very near to you at this moment.' He was
tiring quickly but I could sense that something more than
words entered him at that moment. The next day, at his
request, I brought him Communion. He renewed his baptism
vows and placed his destiny, in life and death, into the hands
of Christ. I read the words of Paul to him, 'your life is hidden
with Christ in God.' And in that faith, on Christmas Eve,
he died.

Young prince

Modern portrayals of the crucifixion have tended to dwell
on the human sufferings and agonies of Christ. What is divine
has become completely absorbed in the awful sufferings of
humanity. But there is also a current of purposeful and irre-

sistible strength running through the whole story. The picture is not complete without it. Early Christian art portrayed Christ as the glorious victor, robed and reigning from his cross as from a throne.

The earliest poem in the English language is about the cross. It is called 'The Dream of the Rood' and the first record of it dates from the year 700, carved on a rood in Dumfriesshire. It is a vision that reflects on the meeting of human weakness and divine might in the crucifixion. The story is told by the cross, the rood. The cross itself, suffering and bending under the weight of sorrow and pain, becomes the broken humanity of Jesus.

> I saw the Lord of all mankind
> Make haste, eager to ascend me.
> When I saw the earth's face shake,
> I dared not break
> Nor bend against the Lord's command.
> I might have laid low all his foes
> Yet fast and firm I stood.
> The young man then unclothed himself,
> Who was God Almighty, strong and brave,
> And there in sight of all who watched,
> High-hearted climbed the cruel cross.
> I shuddered when the man embraced me,
> I dared not bend or fall to earth
> But must stand solid, fast and firm.
> I, a cross, was raised up high,
> And bore aloft the mighty King,
> The Lord of heaven, nor dared hold back.
> They drove dark nails hard through me,
> Made wounds of hatred visible in me
> Gaping gashes of malice;
> I dared not do them harm.
> They mocked, insulted us together,
> And I was moist with oozing blood

Begotten from the young man's side
When he had set free his soul.[1]

'The Dream of the Rood' tells the story of the cross in the
style of the ancient sagas, epic battles and riddles of Anglo-
Saxon times. Christ is the young warrior king who comes
to win our deliverance. No one forces him onto the cross,
he climbs there onto the cross – almost leaps up onto it –
strong and resolute. He delivers and wins the hero's victory
suffering mortal wounds in so doing. The poem is believed
to have inspired the hymn 'When I survey the wondrous
cross'. The second line of this hymn originally read 'Where
that young prince of glory died'.

The harrowing of hell

Very early in the teachings of the Church came the belief
that Christ in death descended into hell itself and laid it waste.
The harrow is the farm implement used to break up rocks,
level the land and prepare the ground for new sowing. The
harrowing of hell is the ancient belief that Christ descended
into hell and broke its gates, tore down its walls, levelled its
kingdom for ever and led its prisoners out of the shadows
into the light of the living.

In a brief reference St Peter teaches that Christ 'was put to
death in the body but made alive by the Spirit, through
whom also he went and preached to the spirits in prison who
disobeyed long ago' (1 Pet. 3:19–20). Notice that it is not the
virtuous dead that Christ goes to.

Medieval imagination vividly pictured the arrival of Christ
in hell, and loved to picture Hades (the gatekeeper of hell)
conned into receiving a mortal body only to discover it was
divine and alive.

Hades was embittered when it tasted of his flesh
It received a body, and it encountered God.
It received earth, and came face to face with heaven.
O death where is thy sting? O Hades, where is thy victory?[2]

Yet the doctrine of hell is a difficult one for many people today. In the first instance there is a contradiction in the belief that eternal punishment is final separation from God. Since God is Life itself there can be no place, even a hell, where he is not. Perhaps we should speak of hell as non-existence. C. S. Lewis suggests that 'there are only two kinds of people in the end: those who say to God "Thy will be done", and those to whom God says, in the end, "*Thy* will be done".'[3] Asked if he believed in hell, Graham Greene once said that for him 'God's love keeps getting in the way of his justice. Hell may be necessary, but I don't think there's anybody in it'.[4]

But there are people in it. Before we speculate on the existence of an underworld, we must face the fact that hell is a present reality in this life for many on earth. The struggle for life and death is not to be confined to some remote speculation about an end-time. In the midst of this world there is a living and dying without redemption or justice and the innocent and oppressed cry continually without release.

On his release after four years as a hostage in Lebanon, Brian Keenan described the experience in these unforgettable words:

There's a silent, screaming slide into the bowels
of ultimate despair.
Hostage is a man hanging by his fingernails
over the edge of chaos
and feeling his fingers slowly straightening.
Hostage is the humiliating stripping away
of every sense and fibre
of body mind and spirit

that make you what you are.
Hostage is a mutant creation,
full of self loathing, guilt and death-wishing
but he's a man –
a unique and beautiful creation
of which these things are no part.[5]

The teaching of Peter makes it clear that hell is a place where Christ is at work proclaiming his word and working to liberate. How do we picture this? Does he preach among the suffering spirits in the darkness of Auschwitz? Do the mass graves of the starving in Sudan or the massacred Kurds in Iraq hear his voice? Can *these* bones live? The Christian Church is called to carry its cross into the heart of these questions. Part of our experience in this world will be to follow Christ into the darkness. The extraordinary advice to one Christian saint at least jumps into focus, 'Put thy mind in hell and despair not'. When Jesus declares Peter to be the rock on which he will build his church he goes on, 'and the gates of Hades will not overcome it. I will give you the keys of the kingdom of heaven; whatever you bind on earth will be bound in heaven and whatever you loose on earth will be loosed in heaven' (Matt. 16:18–19). The life of the church on earth is to be an assault on hell and its every claim upon the world.

The gate of heaven

. . . they shall awake as Jacob did, and say as Jacob did, 'Surely the Lord is in this place', and 'this is no other but the house of God, and the gate of heaven'.[6]

This is our paradox in the face of death. We must accept it as the truth of our mortality. We are dust and to dust we shall return. Life itself cannot begin while death is denied. But we must also protest the claims of death upon us. We were never intended for such a final separation. Christ on the cross declares this: 'He opened wide his arms for us on the cross; he put an end to death by dying for us'. And look into the tomb. God cannot die! Whose death do you see there?

This is a glorious and fearful truth. Our coming to trust and believe in it will be hard won and different for each of us. But we will all one day have testimony of it. For Dietrich Bonhoeffer, writing from the confinement of the prison cell that was his final home on earth, death was a reality to welcome and celebrate – the last 'station on the road to freedom': 'Come now, thou greatest of feasts on the journey to freedom eternal; death, cast aside all the burdensome chains, and demolish the walls of our temporal body, the walls of our souls that are blinded, so that at last we may see that which here remains hidden.'[7]

From Canon John Poulton, late chairman of the Lee Abbey Council, comes a gentler testimony. He suffered ill health for much of the last years of his life and was close to death a number of times. Out of his experience he could write: 'Death is very natural when you get there . . . so welcoming and warm, assuring of well-being. It means home and it feels like home when you get there. I, for a little while, stood in the doorway and I know what it is like.'

PART D

The Wildness of God

'he is not here, he is risen!'

13

A Rumour of Angels

Early on the first day of the week, while it was still dark, Mary Magdalene went to the tomb and saw that the stone had been removed from the entrance. (John 20:1–2)

Looking among the dead

The resurrection was a complete surprise. No one was expecting it. It wasn't planned for. We easily forget that as week by week we recite in our creed that we believe 'in the resurrection of the dead'. Unlike the first disciples we know how the story ended. But for those who lived through that weekend Jesus was dead. His followers were frightened and shattered by what had happened. The body was buried and the crowds had gone home. After a Sabbath day's rest, Jerusalem was about to start another week. No one was expecting any different.

But in a small private garden just outside the city, something had happened in the night. St Matthew says there was a dramatic earthquake and an angel rolled the heavy stone away from the mouth of the tomb (28:2). But the other three gospels simply record that when the women came at dawn

to anoint the body of Jesus, the tomb was open and empty.
If there was an earthquake in the night it doesn't seem that
anyone heard it (except the guards at the tomb – Matt. 28:4).
Isn't it strange that something as dramatic and important as
the resurrection of Christ from the dead should happen without anyone knowing about it? If we had been staying in
Jerusalem that night we would have slept through it all. We
would have woken on the Day of Resurrection to just another
Monday morning!

A DAY LIKE ANY OTHER

it begins like any other,
somewhere in the half light
                    a dog barks
                    a beggar wraps again
against the cold,
an early traveller coughs into
the damp morning air,
somewhere a shutter swings.
                    a city
                        on the edge of waking.

a hint of mist,
of hanging smells
                    of trees and bread
and rotting things.

somewhere a bird stirs
in the first rising colours
of daybreak.

it begins like any other.
                    somewhere near
is a garden with a tomb
that has no stone across it.

it is a day like any other.
soon the traders will rise
and markets fill a day
of heat
with noise and bustle.

it is a day like any other.
                              resurrection
breaks upon us
on a day like any other
we will simply rise from sleep
to discover it.
long before our sleepy hands
have made their mark upon it
                              it is transfigured

the faintest breeze and
                              somewhere
still only half awake
              a rumour of angels.

Unconfined life

Jesus, the 'first born from among the dead', rose from the
tomb in the same way that he was born into this earthly life
– in the middle of the night, hidden from public gaze. No
thunder and lightning and victory celebrations. Once again
the event was shared with the most unlikely and startled
witnesses. And once again angels were on hand to oversee
and guide. It would be very curious to know how God would
have handled the obsessive curiosity of the media in our day
and age.

In the days and weeks that followed the resurrection we
find him quietly meeting individuals and groups of his followers. Each meeting had a purpose. When he came to his

disciples, his words and presence always perfectly matched their situation and their needs.

His first task was to convince them that he was truly alive. Among frightened disciples in the Upper Room he ate fish to show he was not a ghost (Luke 24:41–3). He confronted Thomas's doubts (John 20:24–9). Unrecognised, he walked with two disciples to Emmaus (and in so doing became one of those rare people who hear their own obituaries!). He taught them from the Old Testament, showing them how everything pointed to his dying and rising (Luke 24:13–35).

There was a new elusiveness and mystery about him though. He could appear and withdraw at will. He was unconfined by walls or time and space. And whenever he appeared he was never recognised until he revealed himself by a word or action. In contrast to his silent submission on the way to the cross everything now emphasised his total freedom and authority. The initiative was all his.

An interesting line in the Anglican Communion service takes this further. We thank God that Christ 'revealed the resurrection by rising to new life'.[1] It doesn't say that he achieved the resurrection. The implication is that resurrection itself was never in any doubt. Death was never going to hold Christ captive. What is new is that we are being included. Resurrection is a secret God has known all along and now he is sharing it with us. To put it another way: the stone was not rolled away to let Jesus out. The stone was rolled away *to let us in*.

So what kind of resurrection was revealed to the first disciples?

He is not here

It seems obvious to say it, but their first experience of resurrection was emptiness. They found themselves staring into the dark. The tomb was empty. Jesus was missing. Their expectations were shattered. When, last Easter, some members of my local church complained how hard they found it emotionally to switch from the darkness of Holy Week and Good Friday to the light and joy of Easter Day I felt we were sharing a little in the trauma of those first disciples. It is a strange paradox that our first experience of resurrection may seem to be the loss of God.

I remember talking to a man who had enjoyed a secure and comfortable life. His Christian faith was real and sincere. Then events around him – redundancies at work, illness at home – jolted him to ask bigger questions than he had asked before. The result disturbed him deeply. He described how the faith and convictions that had previously felt firm and secure now felt broken into and ransacked. The part of his life he thought contained belief and 'God' was suddenly empty. He was left staring into darkness wondering where it had all gone. Like Mary he found himself saying, 'They have taken away my Lord and I don't know where they have put him' (John 20:2). And I remember thinking as he quoted that verse, 'but she said those words on Easter Sunday!'

This 'loss of God' is the experience of all faith that is willing to grow and deepen. Because God is God, he must constantly break out of the confines of our limiting beliefs and images of him. George Appleton expressed this in a beautiful meditation based on the experience of Mary beside the empty tomb.

> O Christ, my Lord, again and again I have said with Mary Magdalene, 'they have taken away my Lord and I do not know where they have laid him'. I have been desolate and alone. And thou hast found me again, and I know that what has died was not thou, O Lord, but only my idea of thee, the image I have made to preserve what I have found and to be my security. I shall make another image, O Lord, better than the last. That too must go, and all successive images, until I come to the blessed vision of thyself, O Christ, my Lord.[2]

The resurrection of the body

When they did meet Jesus they met solid flesh and blood. The gospels insist on this and their accounts have all the vividness of eye-witnesses.

I recently led a discussion group on the resurrection. The group was made up of people at all stages of Christian belief and unbelief and I expected a hard time trying to defend the traditional doctrine of the resurrection. But the first contributor not only defended the physical resurrection of Jesus – she did so on scientific grounds.

'As a scientist I have no problem in believing Jesus rose with the same, yet transformed human body. Take carbon for example. Carbon forms the backbone of life – it is found in our proteins, carbohydrates, fats, cells, organs and in coal and oil etc. Pure carbon exists in two forms – diamond and graphite. The atoms are exactly the same in both forms but they are put together differently and are therefore spectacularly different. Diamond is hard, colourless, and crystalline. It is impervious to heat, unbreakable, sparkles in the light and doesn't conduct electricity. Graphite is soft, flaky and feels slippery to the touch. It has a grey, matt surface (rather like coal) and it conducts electricity. If diamond and graphite, essentially the same substance, can exist in such totally contrasting forms I can believe that in the resurrection of Christ we have the same body and human nature, yet totally transformed.'[3]

The Church today has given the impression it is rather embarrassed to believe this or even that it doesn't really matter. But it is vitally important. It means that resurrection is not something we hope for on the other side of this earthly life. In his own resurrection Jesus did not leave behind his human body. He rose with it glorified. He refused to divide spirit from flesh. By his rising he lifted all physical life, body and spirit, giving it a new potential, new hope and dignity.

It is no coincidence that the hunger for prayer and spirituality in our society in recent years has led to a rediscovery of the importance of the body (and of physical creation in general). For so long we treated ourselves as no-bodies when we came to God. In church we carelessly parked our actual bodies on to hard pews and solid kneelers and ignored the discomfort. We even secretly believed there was something virtuous about praying while in pain! But through creative movement, awareness of posture and even simple breathing exercises many people have made the discovery of the power and sensitivity of our physical bodies to share in and mediate spiritual life.

Rubem Alves summed it up like this:

> The Christians included a strange declaration in their Creed. They said they believed in and wished for the resurrection of the body. As if the body were the only thing of importance. But could there be anything more important? Could there be anything more beautiful? That's the way it is: in this body, so small, so ephemeral, the whole universe lives, and if it could, it would surely give its life for the world. God's desire is revealed in our body.
>
> But a strange thing happened. Something tempted us, and we began to look for God in perverse places. We thought to find God where the body ends; and we made it suffer and transformed it into a beast of burden, fulfiller of commands, machine for labour, enemy to be silenced, and we persecuted it in this way to the point of eulogizing death as the pathway to God, as if God preferred the smell of the tomb to the delights of paradise. And we became cruel, violent, we permitted exploitation and war. For if God is found beyond the body, anything can be done to the body.[4]

His hands and his side

For all this I have never come easily to the resurrection of
Jesus. I would have been one of the disciples the angel had
to challenge at the tomb: 'why are you looking among the
dead for one who is alive?' I would have wanted to look
back to the way I remembered him, because my fear is that
in his rising, Christ has left me behind. Resurrection feels
like a super league of life to which I will never gain promotion and I am never comfortable in churches that have
somehow gained promotion. But for people like me, the
risen body of Christ revealed something quite unexpected.

His physical body was still wounded. Isn't that strange?
You would expect a resurrection body to be perfect. Isn't
this a body that has overcome suffering, sin and the grave?
It should no longer carry the blemishes of earthly life – let
alone the scars of pain and death. But not only was the risen
body of Christ still scarred, it was through those scars that
the disciples recognised him – 'he showed them his hands
and his side. The disciples were overjoyed when they saw
the Lord' (John 20:20).

Had Christ risen with a perfect body what hope could that
give us? Such a resurrection cannot be for us in all our tainted
mortality. But if there is resurrection for a body still scarred
and wounded there is hope for us all. In his own body we
see the sign that something new has begun among us. He is
the first born of a new age. The writer of Colossians says it
very simply, 'He is the beginning' (1:18).

Some years ago a missionary doctor in India visited a
remote leper colony. After treating them as best he could he
was asked to preach at their weekly Christian service. He felt
helpless in the face of such suffering. What message could
speak to their experience? Until AIDS, no disease has carried
such stigma and revulsion as leprosy. These people were
social outcasts. The ravages of the disease had left many of
the patients horribly disfigured.

He noticed how they hid their faces and were ashamed of their bodies. He began, hesitantly, to speak about the hands of Christ. He told them of the hands that worked the wood of the carpenter's shop, making smooth and beautiful what was rough and unfinished. He spoke of the hands that blessed and touched the outcast, hands that healed the diseased and the dying. He described the hands that broke bread at the Last Supper – a sign of his suffering to come. Then he spoke of those same hands stretched out on the cross, smashed by hammers, broken and nailed. Now, as he spoke of this suffering love, he noticed some movement among his listeners. Many had horribly crippled hands and they kept them hidden. But now they were looking at their own hands. Such actions spoke of a new self-acceptance. A new dignity. They had found in the wounds of Christ their own wounds. The risen Christ had appeared to them and shown them his hands and his side. And they had recognised him.

14

The Weight of Liberty

The disciples went back to their homes, but Mary stood
outside the tomb crying . . . she turned round and saw Jesus
standing there, but she did not realise that it was Jesus.

'Woman,' he said, 'why are you crying? Who is it you are
looking for?' Thinking he was the gardener, she said, 'Sir, if
you have carried him away, tell me where you have put him,
and I will get him.'

Jesus said to her, 'Mary.'

She turned towards him and cried out in Aramaic, 'Rab-
boni!' (which means Teacher).

Jesus said, 'Do not *cling* to me, for I have not yet returned
to my Father. Go instead to my brothers and tell them, "I
am returning to my Father and your Father, to my God and
your God."'

Mary Magdalene went to the disciples with the news: 'I
have seen the Lord!'

(John 20:10–18)

For many people the meeting of Mary and Jesus in the garden
is the most moving of all the stories of the resurrection. It is
easy to picture her standing by the empty tomb, broken with
grief. She turns and sees Jesus, but doesn't recognise him.
She thinks he is the gardener – and there is the deep irony

in this meeting. For Jesus *is* the gardener. Here in the garden, on the first morning of new Creation, is the second Adam. The whole message of this encounter is – the New Day has dawned. Creation is beginning again. All that the first Adam lost, the second Adam has won back.

Just like the first Adam (Gen. 2:19), Jesus now begins by naming his creation: 'Mary'. And in that naming her eyes are opened and she recognises him. She runs to tell the disciples. The story now lurches from the sublime to the ridiculous for, as the other Gospels tell us, no one believed her because she was a woman! (Luke 24:11)

A letting go

But even in the joy of that meeting Jesus drew back in a way that must have hurt and puzzled her – 'don't cling to me'. He insists on space between them. The relationship with the risen Christ will not be the same as before. And like it or not there was now a clear space between Jesus and his disciples. His appearances seem to have been fairly brief and certainly unpredictable. But in the physical sense, the Jesus they had been used to was not there any more. Previously when Jesus went missing, they went and looked for him, outside the town perhaps, or in the desert. But now he was simply not there and there was nowhere to look. They must have longed for things to be the way they were before. 'Couldn't we start again, Lord?' sings Peter in the rock musical, *Jesus Christ Superstar*. But there is no way back. Jesus has not risen in order to restore his presence as it was before (only with more life and power). For Mary and the disciples, resurrection involved being willing to let go of Jesus.

Our experience of human friendship may give us some clues as to what Jesus was asking of Mary and the disciples. For example, a painful lesson of loving is that no relationship can grow unless there is a willingness to live with change.

Change is a fact of life. It is no use trying to cling to the way things used to be.

I remember speaking to a man whose life and marriage were facing very demanding stresses. He could see clearly that both he and his wife would emerge from that time as different people. He knew what he had first loved in her but now he was asking rather fearfully, 'Will I love what she is becoming?'

Equally clearly, when we try to preserve a relationship by fearful or possessive clinging to the other, no real love or life is possible. It becomes a suffocating embrace. The paradox of real love is that it is not expressed in how close we can get to each other. It actually involves learning the right space between each other. While living in a large Christian community I noticed people struggle with this truth over and over again. Many people joined the community with joy and excitement and threw themselves into the life there. But there came a time (it usually took about three months) when the new member experienced depression and insecurity and a loss of identity. They began to ask, 'Who am I in this place?' It was no longer enough to be carried along by the energy of the community itself. They had to learn to develop the space that would make a real relationship with their world possible.

In his relationship with his disciples following the resurrection, Jesus was teaching them a presence that is not possession and absence that is not abandonment. That is the secret of loving, human and divine. And in that 'space' is the paradox we call Christian freedom.

Deserting to God

'If you hold to my teaching,' Jesus said, ' . . . then you will know the truth and the truth will set you free' (John 8:31). The favourite picture of Christian salvation in the New Testament is one of freedom from captivity. Christ has ended the long reign of sin, broken the power of evil and smashed open the gates of death. One of the original meanings of the word 'to save' is 'to be brought into a spacious place'.

There's a kind of defiance about that kind of freedom in a world like ours. At a recent international gymnastics competition a young girl was thrilling the audience with her movements on the beam. Refusing all the limitations of that narrow plank of wood, she rolled, twisted and somersaulted with complete confidence and grace. 'She makes that beam look as wide as a motorway', cried the commentator. That's freedom.

A similar spirit inspired some of the first Christians to call themselves 'deserters for God'. The nickname may have originated from their refusal to fight in the Roman army, but they applied the spirit of the name to the whole of life. In today's world they might have called themselves dropouts. But they were not abandoning the world for some private paradise. They found in their new life the strength to resist the narrow constraints and demands of the world around with all its pressures to conform. Graham Greene agrees that one mark of the true believer must be a 'certain capacity for disloyalty – disloyalty to existing arrangements, to principalities and powers'. St Peter summed up this attitude to life and its place within Christian experience when he wrote, 'Live as free men, but do not use your freedom as a cover-up for evil; live as servants of God' (1 Pet. 2:16).

Karl Rahner once summarised his Christian faith in these words: 'I would like to be a person who is free and can hope, who understands and shows by his actions that he himself is at the mercy of his freedom, a freedom which throughout his life is creating and making him finally what he should be . . . a person who is faithful, who loves, who is responsible.'[1] This is a demanding calling and the signs are that the first Christians found this saving freedom a difficult life to be faithful to. They seemed to need constant reminding that freedom was the very heart of their new identity in Christ. 'It is for freedom that Christ has set us free. Stand firm, then, and do not let yourselves be burdened again by a yoke of slavery' (Gal. 5:1). They weren't the first people in the Bible to be tempted in this way.

The weight of liberty

The people of Israel were once a nation that longed for freedom. They had endured years of increasingly brutal slavery in Egypt. But when their liberation came they found it very hard to live with. After the initial excitement had worn off they found their freedom very demanding. The sun was hot, the journey long and they began to complain and yearn for captivity again. Before freedom came they had never needed to make choices or decisions. Life had no responsibilities, they just followed orders. Their journey in the desert was one of painful self-discovery and maturing. They had lived so long as slaves, as dependent and subservient people, that they had to learn what freedom was. They didn't just need their physical chains struck off. They had to learn a whole new identity of heart, mind and spirit. They had never known any other way of life. As one person wrote, 'it took one night for Israel to come out of Egypt. It took forty years for Egypt to come out of Israel'.

One modern example may help us understand their burden better. At the end of the Second World War, soldiers reached the first concentration camps to liberate them. They threw open the gates, but inside, no one moved. The soldiers found themselves looking at people so crushed by their captivity that they scarcely recognised freedom when they saw it. They had to be led into freedom by the hand.

In *The Earthsea Trilogy*, Ursula le Guinn tells the story of Tenar, the child priestess who is rescued from the Tombs of Atuan. All her short life she had been the slave of an ancient cult devoted to the worship of Death. Now, as she and her rescuer flee, she is tortured by dark dreams and fears. They reach the coast and set sail in a boat: an act that finally breaks the hold of the old life on her.

> 'Now,' he said, 'now we're away, now we're clear, now we're clean gone, Tenar. Do you feel it?'
>
> She did feel it. A dark hand had let go its lifelong hold upon her heart. But she did not feel joy . . . She put her head down in her arms and cried, and her cheeks were salt and wet. She cried for waste of her years in bondage to a useless evil. She wept in pain, because she was free. What she had begun to learn was the weight of liberty. Freedom is a heavy load, a great and strange burden for the spirit to undertake. It is not easy. It is not a gift given, but a choice made, and the choice may be a hard one.[2]

That passage movingly expresses the paradox of freedom. It makes the choice of freedom sound suspiciously like a call to take up our cross. And perhaps it is exactly that.

The truth is that Christian freedom, in the risen life of Christ, is as disturbing as it is exciting. Life has broken out where no life has been before and God is determined to share it with us. Not for the first time in this strange story of the cross, we find ourselves facing a divine mercy, love and acceptance that refuses to treat us as we have learned to think of ourselves – let alone as we deserve. Nothing in life has prepared us for this so we simply don't know where we stand any more. Someone once described this as the 'hell of mercy'. So the same gospel that fills us with hope of new life, awakens in us, simultaneously, our deepest insecurities and fears.

Yoke of slavery

There is nothing like 'being very involved in the church' for
covering up the need to get more directly involved with
God. It is so much easier to measure Christian life by what
we *do* rather than by grace *received*. It is interesting to notice
how the first Christians were tempted to run from freedom
into captivity again. They didn't abandon religion – they got
more involved in it! The 'yoke of slavery' in Galatians was
the temptation to go back to the old security of being circum-
cised. The Colossians were arguing about food and drink
and precise details of what services they should be having
(Col. 2:16). Faced with something as awesome and disturbing
as the God who rises in our body from death, it is not
surprising that we tend to opt for something safer – something we can see and touch and *control*.

God must constantly rise out of the strange, trivial pre-
occupations that so often make up our attempts at organised
religion. And wherever he does so, we may pray that God
will give us the grace, humility and sense of humour to see
it happening. This strange tension was sharply illustrated for
me at the conclusion of one church service. Near the front
of the church a woman knelt in tears, unexpectedly overwhelmed by a new realisation of God's love for her. At the
back of church, at the same time, a row was going on because
someone hadn't organised the coffee rota properly!

It is ironic that we should seek to hide from the freedom
of God's life by chaining ourselves to some part of his church.
But it may help to explain one of the abiding contradictions
of the Christian church. Entrusted with a message of glorious, anarchic freedom, it remains in practice, fiercely resistant
to change. As Richard Holloway suggests: 'It may be because
that tremendous Grace burns up all our categories of right
and wrong that we are so anxious to tame and systematize
it. So much religion is an attempt to tame the madness of
God.'[3]

15

The Fifth Ace

There is mischief in that Easter morning story. I am convinced of it. How can resurrection be other than mischievous? The world that day was wild, bursting with hidden joy, drunk on new life. We are generally so convinced that religion has to be a serious and dignified pursuit that we constantly miss it. I can imagine the angels on Easter morning peering out of the tomb to see the first disciples coming. I can imagine them trying unsuccessfully to keep silent – handkerchieves stuffed in their mouths to hold in the laughter, bursting with excitement in the sheer joy of their secret. I can see them, out of love for ones in grief, just about keeping a straight face for Peter and the others, as they announce the extraordinary news that life has broken through death forever – 'Why do you look for the living among the dead?'

Wild card

One of my favourite poems, by Anne Sexton, expresses this divine mischief when she likens life to having a game of poker with God. The poem begins when she rows her rowing boat to the dock of an island called God. She gets off the boat and God is waiting for her.

'On with it!' He says and thus
we squat on the rocks by the sea
and play – can it be true –
a game of poker.
He calls me.
I win because I hold a royal straight flush.
He wins because He holds five aces.
A wild card had been announced
but I had not heard it
being in such a state of awe
when he took out the cards and dealt.
As He plunks down his five aces
and I sit grinning at my royal flush,
He starts to laugh,
the laughter rolling like a hoop out of His mouth
and into mine,
and such laughter that He doubles right over me
laughing a Rejoice-Chorus at our two triumphs,
Then I laugh, the fishy dock laughs,
the sea laughs. The island laughs,
the absurd laughs.

Dearest dealer.
I with my royal straight flush,
love you so for your wild card,
that untameable, eternal, gut-driven ha-ha
and lucky love.[1]

Wild card

Christians don't usually describe their relationship with God
in terms of gambling. It doesn't seem theologically 'sound'!
But there is nothing trivial in this picture, for Anne Sexton
was someone who often found life a desperate struggle. Life
didn't appear to her to be dealt out fairly to everyone. Given

a reasonable hand of opportunities, skills and openings we may do our best. But in her experience, after everything had been dealt out and the outcome of the game seemed fixed – a fifth ace would appear from nowhere. Like a wild card in a game of poker, God's love would break in and change everything.

The resurrection of Jesus is God's fifth ace. Just when we thought the whole game was over and lost he has appeared and trumped everything. But that's cheating isn't it? It's not fair! Whoever claimed it was? Nothing in the story of the cross is 'fair' and 'just' in any normally accepted sense of the words. It is a monstrous and terrible story of unjust, barbaric cruelty. But life itself isn't fair either and this is the point. God has suffered the worst injustices, all the random 'unfairness' of this life, and then, when everything seemed over and sealed up, he has broken out.

A few years ago I was in Jerusalem for the Easter celebrations. On Easter Saturday I struggled through the crowds to the Church of the Holy Sepulchre for the ceremony of the Holy Fire. This ancient church is believed to have been built over the site of the crucifixion and tomb of Jesus. It was packed with people who had been queuing since before dawn. They were singing, chanting, and banging drums. They had all the vitality and excitement of a football crowd. Then the procession arrived. The origins of this ceremony are a mystery but every year the Patriarch of Jerusalem processes round the tomb with worship and prayers. He then enters the tomb alone and is sealed inside it.

At that point the crowd went silent. A few voices cried out, 'Come, Lord Jesus'. I began to be aware of a spiritual intensity beneath the surface of what was going on. On one side of the tomb was a small round window which contained bundles of taper candles to be lit by the Holy Fire. The silence and tension grew. We seemed to wait a long time and it was hard to know how to pray. Suddenly there was a flicker of flame in the window. Within seconds, it seemed, the cold dark church was ablaze with light as everyone lit their own tapers and waved them high. Everywhere exploded into noise and life. It was a moment of sheer exhilaration. I found myself, in my black cassock, spattered with hot wax, jumping up and down with everyone else and yelling at the top of my voice.

It frankly doesn't worry me where the flame came from in the tomb. As a dramatic parable of resurrection it was unforgettable and I went around for the rest of the day in something of a daze. I have never before, or since, felt so close to the wild, holy joy of risen life.

God on saxophone

I have to confess that when I want to capture something of the wild vitality of resurrection I turn to a jazz record rather than the church. I firmly believe they play jazz in heaven and I do not believe that the Kingdom of God will arrive on earth until somewhere in the Church of England the service of mattins is accompanied by a jazz band. Though it is actually rooted in very strict time and metre, jazz has a wonderful wildness and chaotic freedom about it. It can take you anywhere, and anything can happen. Leading a retreat for clergy recently, I described what I thought God looked like. He is a large black saxophone player wearing a string vest, hanging out of a bedroom window in New Orleans. He is blowing wildly into the night under the full moon. One of those present at the retreat was an artist and now on my sitting-room wall there is a painting of God to match the poem that inspired it.

> I used to think of you
> as a symphony
> neatly ordered
> full of no surprises.

Now I see you as
a saxophone solo
blowing wildly
into the night,
a tongue of fire,
flicking in unrepeated
patterns.[2]

God willing

'Full of no surprises' describes a religion that has tamed its
God. We would never claim to have done that. It happens
most easily through sheer overfamiliarity, when long
repeated words cease to breathe life and inspire no awe.
Though God is named and worshipped there is the weariness
of duty about it. Of course this is a caricature. If only we
were a little more suspicious about what we put ourselves
through in the name of religion. There is an absurdity about
it at times but we will find our salvation in laughter not in
judgement.

lest God should doubt
we met again
and told him of our love

lest love should pall
we met again
and drove it into song

lest we should die
we run our days
on cycles of Eternity

lest we forget
– exchange our fervour for another –

we meet again same
time tomorrow deus volente

by the treadmills of Devotion
we sat down and wept

sing us one of the songs of Zion

we will
same time tomorrow

Behind the sofa

I was recently talking to a couple who wanted to get married in church. As neither were church-goers I pointed out that by doing this they were inviting God to be involved in their lives in a new way. I spoke of Christ's life and teaching and tried to explain briefly the meaning of the cross and the resurrection. It didn't seem to move them much. The point at which they stirred was when I said, 'Of course, if he rose from the dead then he's around now – he's here with us.' The groom only just resisted the urge to check if anyone was behind the sofa. The bride went pale and admitted, 'It sounds a bit spooky'.

And so it should. Only a few minutes before, they had both announced that they believed in God. But they found the idea that this God might be around at all, most disturbing.

The contradiction was completely reversed later that day when I was reading a magazine article about Professor Stephen Hawking, one of the world's leading physicists, author of *A Brief History of Time*.[3] Here is a man who claims he doesn't believe in a personal deity but loves to speak of his research as 'playing with the mind of God'. And in his own inimitable way he finally admits that he is reaching into mystery when he asks, 'What is it that puts *fire* into these equations?' 'Did not our hearts burn within us?' said the disciples who had walked along the Emmaus road without recognising that the stranger beside them was Jesus. The Christian Church always needs reminding that it has no monopoly of resurrection life. The resurrection tells us that God is fearfully and gloriously at large.

Holy fear

In the light of all this it is puzzling to notice where St Mark appears to have ended his Gospel (in the oldest manuscripts). He finishes his story at the moment the women discover the tomb is empty and hear the message of the angels. The last verse reads, 'Trembling and bewildered, the women went out and fled from the tomb. They said nothing to anyone, because they were afraid' (Mark 16:8). So he leaves us with a vague, enigmatic warning that from the tomb something large, wild and untamed has escaped and may be lurking somewhere near!

The 'fear of the Lord' is regarded as rather old-fashioned religion these days. It is felt to be unhealthy or neurotic. But here before the empty tomb of Christ, before the angels and the mystery of their message, it is common sense if nothing else. For if this story is all it appears to be then something deep and awesome is at work in this world. Above all the resurrection reminds us that we must let God be God and give up all our attempts to tame him.

> O how I fear thee, living God,
> with deepest, tenderest fears
> and worship thee with trembling hope
> and penitential tears.[4]

The fear the Bible speaks of is the ancient dread that all fallen humanity must feel in the presence of Holiness. How could it be otherwise? But far from leaving us cringing and in terror, the Bible says that in the fear of the Lord life finds its true perspective. When God is rightly reverenced and awed at the heart of life, we have begun to get our priorities right. So Isaiah prophesied that the servant of God, filled with his Holy Spirit, would find this fear a liberation and a joy – 'he will delight in the fear of the Lord' (Isa. 11:3). The fear of the Lord is the beginning of resurrection.

Early in the story *The Lion, the Witch and the Wardrobe* the children are given shelter in Narnia by Mr and Mrs Beaver. By the fire, Mr Beaver begins to talk about Aslan, the King of Whole Wood. The children love what they hear and long to meet him, so it is a great shock when they suddenly realise that Aslan is a lion.

> 'Ooh!' said Susan, 'I'd thought he was a man. Is he – quite safe? I shall feel rather nervous about meeting a lion.'
>
> 'That you will, dearie, and no mistake,' said Mrs Beaver; 'if there's anyone who can appear before Aslan without their knees knocking, they're either braver than most or else just silly.'
>
> 'Then he isn't safe?' said Lucy.
>
> 'Safe?' said Mr Beaver; ' . . . Who said anything about safe? 'Course he isn't safe. But he's good. He's the King, I tell you.'[5]

16

A Kind of Love Affair

. . . he sent his servants to tell those who had been invited, 'Come, for everything is ready.' (Luke 14:17)

There is a secret purpose to this whole costly story of the suffering and dying of Christ, and the resurrection reveals it. William Blake described it as 'uniting the form of heaven with the energy of hell'.[1] 'For God was pleased to have all his fulness dwell in him, and through him to reconcile all things, whether things on earth or things in heaven, by making peace through his blood, shed on the cross' (Col. 1:19–20). But what have earth and heaven in common? What has darkness to do with light? A marriage of such opposites would be dismissed as incompatible. Yet a marriage is exactly how the Christian Church describes it.

On Holy Saturday night, in the vigil that celebrates the resurrection of Christ, the liturgy proclaims 'Exsultet':

> This is the night when Jesus Christ
>   vanquished hell
> and rose triumphant from the grave.

> This is the night when all who believe in him

> are freed from sin,
> and restored to grace and innocence.
>
> Most blessed of all nights
> when wickedness is put to flight
>   and sin is washed away,
> lost innocence regained,
>   and mourning turned to joy.
>
> Night truly blessed,
>   when heaven is wedded to earth
> and all creation reconciled to God![2]

So the world is a wedding, the tomb has become a bridal chamber. Christ is the bridegroom and the world his bride. Resurrection is the consummation of the marriage of heaven and earth.

Strange object of desire

The intimacy of this imagery is startling and even offensive to many Christians today. I remember hearing a visiting Russian Orthodox priest being angrily criticised at an ecumenical conference after speaking of the resurrection in this way. Yet it seems that not all our ancestors in the faith shared our inhibitions in this context. It is interesting to note that by the end of the Middle Ages more commentaries had been written on the Song of Songs – a glorious celebration of erotic love – than any other book in the Bible.

'Happy is the one who has no less a desire for God than that of a lover crazy about his beloved', wrote St John of the Ladder, on Mount Sinai. But we won't hear that kind of encouragement in many Christian sermons today. For this is the language of sexual desire and passion and we have come to see our sexuality as the enemy of holiness. So we treat it as something that needs controlling and taming. But we do so at the expense of our ability to love at all. 'There is in passion, a power that holiness needs', wrote Louis Lavelle.[3]

But it is a struggle to believe that we can be the object of such divine desire. When we see someone we don't find particularly attractive receiving love and devotion, we are tempted to ask, 'But what does she see in him?' We might ask the same of God. 'What does he see in us?' We tend to think that most of our struggles with faith are because we don't love God enough. Our real difficulty is in accepting how much he seems to love us. We need a lot of persuading that God could love this world with such passionate longing. Though everything in the ministry of the Christ tells us otherwise, the discovery still surprises us.

Christian believing has come to be so preoccupied with 'being good', self-negating and living up to certain standards that we assume that God can't possibly love us while our lives are in such a mess, or our faith so muddled. Like the disciples we may be unaware of him walking beside us, humble and content to share our lives however dimly recognised.

> Who is the third who always walks beside you
> When I count, there are only you and I together
> But when I look ahead up the white road
> there is always another one walking beside you
> Gliding wrapt in a brown mantle, hooded
> I do not know whether man or woman
> – But who is that on the other side of you?[4]

The perfect fit

The striking thing about the risen Christ is that he spends all his time with weak, unreliable, doubting and rebellious followers. Even at the climax of Matthew's Gospel, when the disciples gathered on the mountain in Galilee to meet Jesus before his ascension into heaven we read, 'they worshipped him – but some doubted' (Matt. 28:17). It seems that believing was no easier for the first disciples than for us and Christ is never revealed so fully as to be obvious.

In fact there are no stories of Christ coming to people who believed with perfect faith and trust – if indeed any such people existed. Instead he made himself known to Mary, broken in her grief; to the stubborn Thomas in his doubts; to Peter who had denied Jesus and gone back to fishing. At each meeting he showed a perfect understanding and acceptance of their struggles. In his persistent, stubborn way he refused to separate the glory of the life of heaven from this frail, wayward humanity. And so each disciple began to awaken to new life through the very wounds and struggles that had made life seem lost to them.

Filling all things

'The Lord is *here*!' is our startling declaration at the start of every service. We are so familiar with it that we forget what an extraordinary claim we are making. We are not surprised to hear those words in church – that is where we expect God to be. But it sounds very different if you stop and say those words in the kitchen or in the middle of the local supermarket.

In *Space for God* I described an experience that brought those words to new life for me. I was working in a parish in North London and my Sunday routine meant an early walk under a grimy railway bridge, down a deserted High Street. It was all drab and grey and covered in litter.

But one particular Sunday I turned into the High Street, and knew it was a holy place. It was the same old road, but God was there. I stopped in my tracks and slowly drank in the realisation that all this dirt and drab greyness was soaked in something holy. It was so improbable. In that Presence everything felt infinitely loved – and infinitely loveable. I wanted to laugh and cry and stay silent all at once. I wanted to dance for joy and hide in fear. But perhaps the most abiding sense of that vision was the realisation that this was no 'special' visit. What I glimpsed in that moment was the longing, abiding Presence that held all of life through its mad, headlong flight – the Presence that we would soon drown out again with the roar of traffic and trampling humanity. It was new to me because previously I had neither the eye nor heart to perceive it. 'Surely the Lord was in this place, and I was not aware of it . . . This is none other than the house of God.'[5]

If the church believes in the resurrection of Christ then its worship will always have a certain madness about it. For whatever the evidence to the contrary, Christian faith insists on viewing the world from a quite different perspective. It claims that the evidence of our eyes is not the whole story, and that what we don't yet see is the greater reality. Above all, it stubbornly refuses to separate heaven and earth any more. They are now united in the love of Christ. What once belonged in heaven is now the life of earth as well.

> Holy, holy, holy,
> God of power and might,
> Heaven *and earth* are full of your glory
> Hosanna in the highest.[6]

The energy of hell

But how do we respond to such a gospel as this? To know the life of heaven we need the energy of hell. Our believing will need all the passion and wildness that has been too long denied to Christian faith.

While working as a missionary among the Masai people in East Africa, Vincent Donovan struggled to know how to translate what it was 'to believe' into their language. He finally chose a word that many of us would have opted for – it literally meant 'to agree to'. But a Masai elder confronted him with advice that changed his whole understanding of faith.

> He said that 'to believe' like that was similar to a white hunter shooting an animal with his gun from a great distance. Only his eyes and his fingers took part in the act . . . for a man really to believe is like a lion going after its prey. His nose and eyes and ears pick up the prey. His legs give him the speed to catch it. All the power of his body is involved in the terrible death leap and single blow to the neck, the blow that actually kills. And as the animal goes down the lion envelops it in his arms, pulls it to himself, and makes it part of himself. That is the way a lion kills. This is the way a man believes. This is what faith is.

But the elder had not finished.

> 'We did not search you out, Padri. We did not even want you to come to us. You searched us out. You followed us away from your house into the bush, into the plains, into our hills, into our village. You told us of the High God, how we must search for him, even leave our land and our people to find him. But we have not done this. We have not left our land. He has searched *us* out and found us. All the time we think we are the lion. In the end, the lion is God.'[7]

The feast of life

Jesus too spoke of faith as an asking, a searching, a seeking out – it is our part of a mutual pursuit that must take everything we can give. And whenever Jesus wanted to describe the reward of such faith – the love of God – he told stories of banquets, parties and celebrations. It is no coincidence that the first miracle he performed was at a wedding where he transformed a celebration that had run dry with the miracle of water into wine – and in very large quantities at that.

And it was through a special meal that he chose to leave his followers a sign that would forever express his dying and rising for the world. 'This is my body, given for you' – the love of God willing to suffer, to be broken and consumed by the world.

But before Communion is shared the church hears these words of invitation:

> Jesus is the Lamb of God who takes away the sin of the world, happy are those who are called to his supper.

The second line comes from the climax of the book of Revelation. The supper we are invited to, that has all the marks of a mournful memorial, has actually become a wedding banquet.

> Hallelujah, for the Lord God Almighty reigns.
> Let us rejoice and be glad
> and give him glory!
> For the wedding of the Lamb has come,
> and his bride has made herself ready.
>
> (Rev. 19:6–7)

Do you know the story of *Babette's Feast*? It is set in an isolated rural community on the coast of Denmark. It was a deeply religious community but their pastor had died some years before and the spirit and joy had long gone from their life together. There was bitterness and resentments among them and their lives were as mean and frugal as they assumed heaven to be. One night a stranger arrived. She was an exile from the French Revolution and had no money. Her name was Babette and they gave her shelter and she cooked for them. Before long they could hardly remember how they ever managed without her.

Babette's only link with her distant home was a lottery ticket and one day she heard that she had won a very large sum of money with it. She offered to cook the villagers a special meal on the anniversary of their religious founder. Very nervously, they agreed, not knowing that the feast would be so extraordinary that it would cost Babette everything she had.

As the day drew near, strange food and provisions arrived from distant places. It made that insular community nervous and insecure. So much so that they wondered if they had agreed to a witch's feast.

When all was ready they came to the feast so fearful of its power that they had secretly vowed not to enjoy it. But this was food and drink such as they had never tasted before. A visiting general was eating with them. His life too had become rigid with denial and secular ambition. He knew nothing of their pact and the power of the food awakened memories and joy in him. He remembered a chef in Paris who 'was capable of turning a feast into a kind of love affair, in which physical and spiritual appetites could not be distinguished'. That chef was Babette.

But now the villagers themselves were being changed by what they shared. They began to smile and laugh and forgive again. Their voices softened as they spoke to each other with new caring. Hands touched with tenderness, something lost long ago being rediscovered. The meal had become a kind of love affair.

At the end of the feast the general stood and spoke these words:

'Mercy and truth are met together
Righteousness and peace shall kiss each other.'
Man in his weakness and short sightedness believes he must make his choice here in life, and fears the risk he runs.

We tremble, but no . . . our choice is meaningless
The time will come when our eyes will be opened
and we shall see that mercy is without end.
We shall wait in trust and remember with gratitude
Mercy imposes no conditions
And see, all that we have chosen, is granted to us
All we have refrained from . . . is permitted
Indeed we also get back that which we have cast away.
'Mercy and truth are met together,
Righteousness and peace shall kiss each other.'[8]

Late that night one of the last villagers left the house. He
swayed happily in the darkness, drunk, but not only from
wine. Standing by the village well he lifted his head, thrust
out his hands under the wide, starry sky and cried, 'Hallel-
ujah!'

Notes

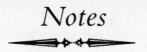

Monsignor Quixote's Dream
1. Graham Greene, *Monsignor Quixote* (Penguin 1982), pp. 76–7.

PART A: OPEN ARMS

Chapter 1: Divine Welcome
1. *Alternative Service Book* (Clowes/SPCK 1980), p. 136.
2. Ibid. p. 499.
3. *Peter Abelard* (The Reprint Society 1950), pp. 268–70.

Chapter 2: Strange Fruit
1. Sinclair-Stevenson 1990.
2. John Stott, *Only One Way* (IVP 1974), p. 179.
3. Quoted in *Lord of the Journey*, A Reader in Christian Spirituality, compiled and edited by Roger Pooley and Philip Seddon (Collins 1986), p. 132.

Chapter 3: Easter Was Late This Year
1. Macrina Wiederkehr, *Seasons of Your Heart* (Silver Burdett Company 1979), pp. 121–2.

Chapter 4: Standing in the Breach
1. My grateful thanks to Bishop Stephen Verney for permission to use this picture of the cross, and to Suzanna Rust for making the new drawing.
2. *Alternative Service Book*, p. 144.
3. Quoted in *Lord of the Journey*, p. 136.

PART B: THIS IS MY BODY

Chapter 5: Love Fore-given
1. Quoted in *Christian Aid Newspaper*, April 1984.
2. *Prayer* (Veritas Publications 1974), p. 82.
3. Jim Cotter, *Prayer at Night* (Cairns Publications 1988), p. 79.

Chapter 6: This Side of Heaven
1. Adapted from John Peters, *Frank Lake – the Man and His Work* (DLT 1989), p. 121.
2. *The Drama of Being a Child* (Virago 1986), p. 30.
3. Rowan Williams, quoted by Martin Smith in *A Season for the Spirit* (Fount 1991), p. 78.
4. Jim Cotter, op. cit., p. 65.
5. My poem, as are those on pp. 112 and 131.

Chapter 7: O Happy Fault!
1. Cited in K. Leech, *True God* (Sheldon Press 1985), p. 300.
2. *Alternative Service Book*, p. 120.
3. SCM 1981, p. 87.
4. Ibid. p. 86.
5. *God of Surprises* (DLT 1985), pp. 74–5.

Chapter 8: The Sign of Jonah
1. Richard Holloway, *Consecration*, from the text of an address given at Catholic Renewal Conference, Loughborough, 1980.
2. *I Believe in the Resurrection of the Body* (Fortress Press 1986), p. 7.
3. Sheldon Press 1976, p. 362.

PART C: WHOSE DEATH DO YOU SEE THERE?

Chapter 9: The Forsaken Night
1. *Night* (Penguin 1981), p. 73.
2. *Good Friday People* (DLT 1991), p. 114.
3. From a poem by former Beirut hostage, Brian Keenan. Full text appears on pp. 105–7.
4. A version of this story is told by Laurens Van der Post, *Testament to the Bushmen* (Penguin 1985), p. 139.

Chapter 10: The Wounds of Loving

1. Cited by Robert Fisk, *Pity the Nation* (OUP 1991), p. 394.
2. Kenneth Leech, *True God* (Sheldon Press 1985), p. 316.
3. From C.M.S. Lent Project material, 1991.
4. Made famous by a song of the same name, by rock musician, Sting.
5. *My Name Is Asher Lev* (Penguin 1972), pp. 287–8.

Chapter 11: Against the Grain

1. Margaret Craven (Picador 1980), pp. 34–6.
2. Mandarin 1990.
3. Cited in Alan Jones, *Soul Making* (SCM 1985), p. 72.

Chapter 12: The Bones

1. I am grateful to Anna Kingston for this translation from the Anglo-Saxon and to Bishop Simon Barrington-Ward for introducing me to the poem in an address and discussing it further in recent correspondence.
2. Cited in *Good Friday People*, p. 154.
3. Cited in *Lord of the Journey*, p. 383.
4. In conversation with Antony Burgess, *Homage to Qwert Yuiop (Selected Journalism 1978–85)* (Hutchinson 1986), p. 24.
5. Read at a news conference upon his release, 30 August 1990 and quoted in *The Independent* newspaper the following day.
6. Cited in *Lord of the Journey*, p. 377.
7. *Letters and Papers from Prison* (SCM Press 1976), p. 371.

PART D: THE WILDNESS OF GOD

Chapter 13: A Rumour of Angels

1. *Alternative Service Book*, p. 136.
2. Quoted in Michael Hollings and Etta Gullick, *The One Who Listens* (Mayhew-MacCrimmon 1971), p. 153.
3. My thanks to Catrin Morgan for probably the first science lesson I have ever enjoyed.
4. *I Believe in the Resurrection of the Body*, pp. 8–9.

Chapter 14: The Weight of Liberty
1. Cited in Alan Jones, *Soul Making*, p. 8.
2. Penguin 1982, p. 295.
3. Cited in Philip Seddon, *Darkness* (Grove Spirituality Booklet No. 5), p. 5.

Chapter 15: The Fifth Ace
1. From 'The Rowing Endeth', *The Complete Poems* (Houghton Mifflin Company 1982), pp. 473–4.
2. 'Spiritus' by Steve Turner, *Up to Date* (Hodder 1982), p. 166.
3. Bantam 1978.
4. 'My God, how wonderful thou art', *With One Voice Hymnbook* (F. F. Faber, Collins 1977).
5. C. S. Lewis (Puffin Books 1960), pp. 74–5.

Chapter 16: A Kind of Love Affair
1. Cited by John Sanford, *Ministry Burn-out* (Arthur James Ltd 1982), p. 95.
2. *Lent. Holy Week. Easter Services and Prayers* (Church House Publishing 1986), p. 231.
3. Both quotations in this paragraph cited by Martin Smith, *A Season for the Spirit* (Fount 1991), p. 73.
4. T. S. Eliot, 'The Wasteland', *The Complete Poems and Plays of T. S. Eliot* (Faber and Faber 1969), p. 7.
5. Daybreak, DLT 1990, p. 135.
6. *Alternative Service Book*, p. 131.
7. *Christianity Rediscovered* (SCM 1984), pp. 62–3.
8. The General's speech is a transcription from the English subtitles to the film. For an extended reflection on this theme see Rubem Alves' wonderful book, *Poet, Warrior, Prophet* (SCM 1990), chapters 1 and 6.

Thanks are due to the following for permission to quote copyright material: Cairns Publications from *Prayer at Night* by Jim Cotter; HarperCollins Publishers from 'Terribly Familiar' from *Seasons of the Heart* by Macrina Wiederkehr (reprinted 1991 © 1991 Macrina Wiederkehr); Hodder & Stoughton Ltd from 'Spiritus' from *Up to Date* by Steve Turner; Sterling Lord Literistic Inc. from 'The Rowing Endeth' from *The Complete Poems* by Anne Sexton.